Grimspound AND

ROD MENGHAM's published poetry includes *Chance of a Storm* (Carcanet, 2015), *Unsung: New and Selected Poems* (Salt, 2001), *Parley and Skirmishes* (Ars Cameralis, 2007) and with Marc Atkins a book of texts and film stills, *Still Moving* (Veer, 2014). He has published monographs and edited collections of essays on nineteenth- and twentieth-century fiction, violence and avant-garde art, the 1940s, and contemporary poetry. He has co-edited the anthologies *Altered State: The New Polish Poetry* (2003) and *Vanishing Points: New Modernist Poems* (2005). His translations include Andrzej Sosnowski's *Speedometry* (Contraband, 2014).

Grimspound

AND

Inhabiting Art

ROD MENGHAM

CARCANET

C Λ R C Λ N E T

First published in Great Britain in 2018 by
Carcanet
Alliance House, 30 Cross Street
Manchester M2 7AQ
www.carcanet.co.uk

A CIP catalogue record for this book is
available from the British Library,
ISBN 978 1 78410 590 7

Typeset by Andrew Latimer in Joanna Nova
Printed in Great Britain by SRP Ltd., Exeter, Devon

The publisher acknowledges financial
assistance from Arts Council England.

Contents

GRIMSPOUND   7
   Part 1   9
   Part 2   25
   Part 3   41
   Part 4   57
A Note on Grimspound   70

INHABITING ART   71

Acknowledgements   255

Grimspound

I

I FIRST CAME TO GRIMSPOUND in winter, in ignorance. Having parked the car, I stepped away from it and listened. There was the sound of a distant jet engine, slowly fading and gradually converting into the sound of Grimslake, the stream that runs through one quarter of Grimspound in its descent to the valley floor. The water was plunging and pouring down into a small pebble-knocking gulf; a sound falling into itself over and over again. The stream in winter is torrential, constantly undercutting its own flow, rocking all the stones on its bed, while beneath each successive fall of water, shoals of air bubbles form and re-form, like clouds under a ridge. The volume and velocity of the current creates a transparent scalloping over the broad convexities of the larger shelves of granite on the stream bed. Small channels pulse backwards and forwards across the path that climbs alongside, and in the wettest winters other areas of grass on the hillside are flattened and combed out whenever extra storm vents are needed.

Dry conditions are rare in this season, and I have experienced them only once, in November 2003, when Grimslake had shrunk to a valiant trickle, barely audible and nursing a smoothly terraced effect in the sluicing of water over stone. Here and there, the depleted flow would turn into a stutter, as if intercepted by a valve. After a long dry spell, the sudden rain when it comes loosens and booby-traps the earth, gashing it everywhere with the skid-marks of headlong sheep. When the temperature plunges, the bracken is frayed and ghostly, there are white husks of heather bloom and trails of spiderweb over the densely fossiliferous rock. The small pools of Grimslake have palisades of ice pendants, and the gelid water slides under a frozen cowl, over mossed stones. The wind carries hints of vanilla and tobacco, while tiny flecks of celestial blue minerals appear on the path, small circles of copper-blue lichen. Three mysterious clots of whitish jelly are strewn on the grass.

By Easter-time, the dead bracken is as crisp as straw, and the stream has broken free, it is making a chute near the road. I try to pick out the fretting passage of a small runnel off to one side of the main channel, the beginning of a great shift in the balance. Walking here in spring involves a series of acoustic alterations, a piloting between rising and falling levels of water splash and wind pressure, between the racket of exposed places and the detailed quiet in the lee of a boulder. Crouching down in the shadows, you can see how the exposed water weed has survived under a sheet of gel, trapping the moisture and stopping the green cells from drying out.

By early summer, the rusted tips of the ferns are uncurling, and there are bracken shoots in the middle of the path bearing their standards while others prepare to arch their necks. The first sound of Grimslake is in competition with the wind and the gargling sheep, but each pool in the stream's descent is now deep enough for the water to make a plunging sound. There are tiny yellow quatrefoils dotted along the banks, while the growth of moss on rocky platforms in the stream produces a complex pattern of accelerating and decelerating pulses.

With the lowering of water supply in high summer, there are three distinct notes and volumes in the sound of water falling at separate points. The yellow quatrefoils are flourishing alongside miniature soap bush. Airborne sounds are carried from far and near: a bird unlocking a snail, then a dog barking, seconds before the hurtling fighter jet is heard. By each pool in the stream, reeds grow through overhanging festoons of heather while midget water boatmen scull round each other in a display of aquatic dodgems.

By late summer, there are multiple arches of pale bracken in the path, and no sound of water. Grimslake is silent, the stream-bed dry. In only one place is there a faint throttle and slippage under dense bunches of heather. On the water left in each pool are yellow petals that stay in place, like buoys within a bay. All the vivid green moss has been flattened into dark brown mats of rubber. The insects make hay. It is the season of feathery-headed grasses and drying thistle heads.

On the edge of autumn, Grimslake is completely hushed, with only the sound of moving grasses and washed gravel deposits of tumbled stones to speak of its other life. Gorse flowers are sheltering among the bracken, and adjacent clumps of heather show different shades of green as well as different tones of purple; the same bush might include four distinct purples. The dry earth has loosened stones of red granite thickly veined with mica. Below them are the terraces of vanished waterfalls, now spanned by gleaming spiders' webs beaded with tiny globes of light.

The drama of the stream, its ebbing and flowing, with its stage-set dismantled and reconstructed every year, offers a seasonal equivalent to the much larger rhythms of this series of reflections, and is collateral to its inventions. The drama intensifies, before even the Bronze Age compound has been reached, in the story of a tree and its nest. This ancient, lowly thorn tree, with many fractured limbs now dressed with great plasters of moss, leans over the stream. At the base of the channel where it is bowed, granite boulders are packed round with smaller, less rounded, stones of terracotta colour, and it must be the percolation system these provide which puts life into half the available boughs. Less than eight feet off the ground, the boughs support a great nest swung to and fro in the wind. The nest seems as old as the tree, and indeed the branches in their growth have twisted round and round and round each other, as if in imitation of its structure. In winter, both carry government-issue camouflage of russet and green moss, while in summer there is a flourish of olive pale leaves, advanced on by reconnoitring slugs. Even in the driest spells, the gnarled roots of the thorn are able to detect the faintest rill of fresh water, where the small birds drink. After four years of visiting, I returned to the site one winter to find the nest still there, but showing no sign of refurbishment. Despite this neglect, it was a shock to me, the following year, the shock of disbelief, to have to accept that the nest was finally undone, carried away by winter storms. Without my realising, it had been a sheet-anchor, now no more than a speculative probe, a sign of habitation deleted without trace, the landscape re-forming quickly and irretrievably to forget it. Two years on, and a replacement had been built, with heather roots lined with earth and copper-coloured lichen. I was excited, but this rhythm of uncertainty is now one of the reasons I cannot go back – in itself a strange hesitancy to arise from this compulsion I have to stand among ruins.

I never hesitate over my entry point into the citadel. I use that word because the thought of Mycenae arrived, unbidden, with my first sight of the great, cyclopean stones of the eastern entrance to Grimspound. But I do not use the original gate, steering instead through a gap in the wall-rubble that gives onto an area set aside for a stock-pen. There is a second, much more feral, stock pen in the south-west corner of the site, but that has little power over me. Here, along the main wall of the compound, flat stones have been placed to the interior, giving the impression of having been dressed, and there are always strands of wool clinging to the largest of the level blocks, showing me that sheep still use the pen, out of long habit. Better still, after heavy rain, there are sumps of clear water filling hoof-shapes in the mud, to record the fact that horses also use the area.

Within the compound, the first sound in summer is often that of sheep teeth tearing at the mixed diet of grass and stunted bush. Denuded heather stems lift like timber off a beach. There is the heady thermal smell of bracken roots in peaty soil, an abundant harvest of cuckoo spit on the heather, and sometimes the clean white bone of a sheep. The longer grasses are dried out and wispy: stiff tassels shaking in the wind. The turf is deeply cushioned with tiny infills of moss and small orange mushrooms bleached on top, their colour most intense on the fringe.

Animals are now the only inhabitants, helping to preserve the character of the site, but also knocking it about. I once surprised five horses and two foals gathered around hut circle number three. Their hooves buffering on the turf could be heard clearly from three hundred yards away. This drumming often disturbs the forensic memory of the stones, waiting to reveal the angle of their fall to the absent archaeologist. In the south-west of the compound, between the gate and the stock-pen, in one of the larger hut circles, eight paces across, one of the wall stones has been pushed out of place recently, uncovering a hollow inside the wall, a space closed up for three and a half thousand years, now empty but crossed by brown roots. Sheep and horses have evidently made a breach in the main wall nearby.

Much of the site is now feral. Bundles of reeds are thriving within many hut circles, perhaps descended from spores dropped from shaken-out bedding. Roughly a quarter of the reeds sport mossy outgrowths halfway down the stem. There are several dimensions of growth here. Many of the heather domes are flattened and snapped in parts, the middle stopped up with moss, while mimic heathers, of a softer fabric and a brighter green, colonise the surface of larger bushes. Wherever there is shelter, flourishing wedges of mace-head moss are inserted in every plausible crevice. If you bend down to ground level, you find yourself among tiny Portuguese man-of-war toadstools.

The north-west quadrant now appears clear of hut circles, as if the Bronze Age inhabitants had plans for future development. But there are a few mounds covering stones, and at least one likely construction rising in the centre of this area. The ground in the whole of the north-west quarter is inflated with cold water in winter, the long, exposed heather roots smooth and shiny like seaweed, and it may be that any settlement here would be abandoned after two or three seasons.

Building a hut circle would have required little effort compared to the immense, collective project of the main compound wall. Just south of the course of Grimslake, the rubble spread from this is fifteen or sixteen feet across. The biggest stones remain upright. Several have a rocker shape, tying in with each other. The three largest blocks by the north entrance are long and tapering, as if shaped originally to be standing stones. In the western wall, there is a massive upright showing clearly how it was engineered into place. Behind it, at the bottom of small empty chambers in the foundations, water slips by at regular intervals, every seven seconds. Chambers among the wall-stones are more frequent on this side of the site, where Grimslake has scoured them out. Those to the north, much drier, make lairs for spiders. To the east, they have linings of bracken and dried grass.

The Great Stone of the West is slightly concave, making an obvious back rest, now as then. On my last visit, it was guarding an empty champagne bottle adorned with purple bird droppings. There are blue stains, vertical and horizontal smears, nearly everywhere on the tumbled wall stones. But their colour is insignificant compared to that of the wall itself. The grey skin now covering everything has been left by generations of lichen. A scrape with a pen-knife blade will reveal a glow of pink granite underneath. The original wall must have been a great roseate screen in the morning sun, an astonishing sight. All this is now hidden. On the southern wall there are lime-green bulbs of moss, and many of the horizontal slabs are half covered with up to four inches of peat and gnarled growths of heather, the stems as broad as my thumb. Everything here might be covered, dried out and blown away, hundreds of times. Only the more sulphurous-looking lichens stay the course through thick and thin, on angled stones that have tipped to forty-five degrees.

The wind is almost sonorous in the belt of reeds along the western wall. It is layered with the sound of Grimslake flowing through flutes in the rock. The water rattles the stones underground in unexpected places all around the great western upright. The stones of the wall here are acoustic traps, throwing the sound of chutes in the stream, ventriloquial tricks of the trade. In spring, the reed-beds are abundant, and cresses and mosses are piled over one another at the very edge of the stream. The new growth of reed is almost as high as the dead stems it uses for support. Flow-patterns in the water are serene and orderly, but the vents from the underground passage carrying the stream right into the compound are at their most rowdy. Where the water actually enters the compound it shoots through, and in one place the roof of the underground aqueduct has collapsed, revealing clean pale stones on the bed of the channel. In the larger pools being formed, the entering water creates small plateaux with transparent contour lines refracting the light.

In summer, Grimslake is often reduced to a trickle, and even north-west of the compound, right upstream, nearly all the water has gone, and what is left is filled with larvae. In the winter, this area becomes a great mossy sump, and Grimslake is forced to find many new channels west of the compound. In the pools here, great sacs of bubbles rise like spawn. If you follow Grimslake upstream in winter, it soon becomes a delta, then a marsh, then a quag, and there is no way to trace it back to source. Wherever the flow is faster and deeper, there is more visual distortion, like the flow of time. All along the bank there are flecks of wool going through an endless rinse cycle.

Inside the compound, the water flows through the underground aqueduct, and in winter also over the grass, to meet at a basin with flat stones whose surface lies just above, or just below, the water level, depending on the season. The stones have clearly been placed there for washing clothes, precisely where the stream enters from under the turf, bringing with it distant profound gurglings. Tiny green sashes of weed and slime, bacterial in structure, flail in the current. In winter, the area above the opening becomes a miniature flood-plain, a maze of cross-currents. But when the flow relents, the long tunnel to the washing stones has enough air along its fifty-foot length to carry the echoes of distant rushing and cornering, like a remote cistern always refilling. When the water level is low down in the basin, the great washing stones are exposed to the open air. However, one deep pool is always there, edged with ghostly weed and trails of spawn. One of the largest, flattest stones, when dried out round the base, wobbles under pressure, and this movement releases an inky cloud. One summer, I came across a new black and yellow pencil dropped beside this platform, its leaden point dipped in the main flow.

By far the most spectacular elements of Grimspound life are the mosses and lichens. They are perpetually at war under long slithering streaks of cloud. On the north wall, the seasonal growth in the larger moss colonies is exactly two inches. Later colonies of moss prefer bedding down in their predecessors, showing layers of habitation like the Bronze Age city of Troy, all the way down to the granite bedrock. By contrast, the circles of lichen look like blueprints for a ring cairn. Every return to the site means a different configuration of moss. The discovery of drifts of white coral moss peppering a fallen block outside the north entrance indicates a major shift in migration patterns. While a microscopic spider climbs the trumpet lichen, and several tiny jet beads with legs traverse the moon rock of ossified plant life, entire planets of moss encircle and avoid the prows and nuggets of quartz in the wall stones. Green globular pads of moss slowly put out antennae.

Lichen overcrowding is so acute in the north-west corner, it resorts to limescale methods on any plant that does not resist. Much of the lichen is blackened but silky to the touch. In the south, and facing south, there are many more stones coated with the dry grey scales of old growth. The oldest patches have been calcified into marble entombing the record of their change. Among the more recently established grids are clearings in the lichen forest where an expeditionary force has blasted. In winter, the lichens are damp and spongy. New arrivals are a vivid yellow and as soft to the touch as mustard powder. Among the colonies of old grey matted lichen are streaks of pink ruin where the spores react to a vein of minerals in the rock.

The yellow-green varieties have vertical plates, like food traps on a coral reef. The spongier varieties with complex tendrils seem to be travelling the site like tumbleweed. At the base of one small orthostat is a chalk-pale green specimen with ship's funnels. In the west, there is a small patch blooming into midget wild strawberry heads. And controversy still rages but the soft whitish coral lichen appears to be symbiotic with a bright green starred moss.

The giant blocks of the great gate are covered almost entirely in lichens and moss. Sheltering by the gate during a winter storm, with my shoulder up against studs of quartz in the granite, I contemplate the rich silage underfoot and a few new fragments of red, grey and black stone broken off by the winter weather. The low sun brings out a cross shape carved on the northern flank of the gate and highlights the knobbly outgrowths of tiny succulents bedded down in Lilliputian moss and lichen on the shelf above. The entrance proper under my feet is heavily paved but ends in steps, since there was no use for any wheels anywhere here, only feet and hooves. There are sheep droppings everywhere, most surprisingly on the very top of the gate, where there is absolutely no vegetation, and no shelter, nothing but a good view, the ovine sublime.

Birds are the most frequent visitors. At all points of the compass, kestrels stoop. Sky-diving through wind, they open their wings for a split-second only, each time they stabilise. My eye is caught by the swooping flight of a stonechat, before I hear the tiny rattle of its alarm call, a series of warning clicks. In the spring, a cuckoo-welcome fades up the hill on approach to the site, replaced by the gravelly riff of a bunting with deep pink throat and black crest. In the summer heat, there is often quiet, broken by the clear piping call of the curlew, the chirr of now untroubled stonechats, the urging of a distant cuckoo and, high above all, the pealing cry of the falcon. Into the quiet, one, two, three, four larks speed away from the bed of the stream and dive down into crevices with the velocity of swallows, or miniature gannets. In winter, I am decoyed all the way up Hamel Down by six fieldfares, taking it in turns to lead the way. On coming back down, I try stalking a wren along the south-east wall to find its nest, but the number of boltholes is too confusing, there is increasing soil erosion here, more and more collapse.

Summer is for the insects, and the different tempos of stridulation. Crickets pause and resume dialogues with the sound of nagging sheep, and there are glistening slugs on the move. Flying insects lob themselves onto your shirt, rolled up into small black torpedoes, the first stage in a plan you hasten to cut short. The birds usually make short work of the caterpillars, but occasionally you will find a dead yellow and black striped caterpillar wearing a funereal ruff of rainwater spheres on its furred back.

The ponies are rarely seen in the summer months. It is winter when they tend to come down from the hills and drift towards the roads, harassed by gales. I often find their hoof prints, fringed with a few upthrusting bunches of ice nodules, showing they have been here recently but have moved on, it is too cold. Once in summer, I was climbing the approach path when suddenly there was the quick reek of Dartmoor ponies, twenty one of them including foals, stock still to the north of the path. They watched while a big dog fox crossed the path and paused to look at me. It was 11.10 in the morning.

But humans are the rarest of all visitors. There are voices on the wind, the cries of children, calling from one tor to the next, but I rarely share this space with others. I have grown possessive of it. Certain timbres of voice make me nervous. I reach the great south wall and launch a defender's curse at a file of Ramblers approaching across the valley. As two walkers cross the compound, I cannot help listening to the narrative of a burned child, abandoned by her mother, cherished by her father. The female walker tells the story without judgement, with a careful sense of relevance. And then I have to realise that the conversations of walkers connect with the deepest meanings of this place, with the reported speech and narratives of a knowable community. The great compound walls are the pretext for a shift from lyric to epic, from elemental songs to a larger world of smaller things, of more varied relationships, a range of personalities; and then there is the further shift, to marching songs, the ones that carry you into unknown territory.

Winter is not the marching season here, nor even the walking season. It is when various bits of soft tissue rigidify, vital organs start to freeze into inaction, and the skull becomes a conducting plate for polar extinction. You have to pace yourself, to make your knees last, and the only conversations are with the wind and the sky. Winter sky descends on Grimspound, the first tendrils of cloud hang at the very edge of the settlement. As the wind pounces from one bush of heather to the next, light begins to fail in seconds. The cloud begins to push away all sound. I see the bents stirring but cannot hear what makes them do it. A cold haze brushes over the ridge to the south in a series of festoons when suddenly the bottom drops out of the nearest cloud; a whirling nebula of vapour plunges down in loosening spirals, it powers towards me, and there is no cover.

In summer, the wind as it blows around the body mixes frequencies and volumes in ways that influence each step. Shifting passages of light open up and close between the fast-moving clouds, although there is one pillar of cloud that does not move among the shoals of drifting vapour.

The wind, concussing among the stones of the wall like an erratic motor, blows from all quarters. It beats lightly about my shirt, while the sound of a heavily freighted bee corkscrews into the brain.

Looking south to the next ridge, sunlight pools across the hillside, into small elbow-shaped valleys, and then withdraws, to the ebbing sound of distant earth-movers. There is a ruched blanket of warm air, but always to the west somewhere, a great dark blue cloud. In the middle distance, a single hiker is traversing Hameldown, while clouds pour overhead at five times his rate of progress. On the very top of Hameldown itself, various distances are plumbed by the ear, as the bracken creaks nearby.

At what point did my search for evidence lead out of sight, to the nowhere of the vanishing point? Start with the microscope, then the telescope, then worry about the middle distance. I could not channel all the details, keep them within bounds. The flow of information did not lead back to source, only to a spongy indefiniteness. The series of visits I made began to evolve its own narrative, its own rules of composition. At a certain point it became an obscure necessity to compare Grimspound with its nearest Bronze Age neighbour, the more remote, the more exiguous, Berry Pound. Completely effaced by bracken in summer, completely cut off by waterlogging in winter, Berry Pound can only be reached, and inspected, in spring.

Berry Pound is faintly discernible from the opposite side of the steeply banked valley of the East Wedderburn river. Its perimeter merges with a later field wall that has used up most of its stone. The remaining fragments of compound wall consist of enormous, immovable boulders, many almost totally blackened, although the pigment is only superficial. (Was this fire damage caused by the nearby competitors at Grimspound?) A dried up watercourse runs alongside the north wall, in the manner of Grimslake. The perceptible rubble spread is just as wide as at Grimspound, with a possible gated entrance more or less due north, facing downhill. I have tracked the footings of at least eight hut circles, mainly in the south-west quadrant. (At Grimspound, the greatest settlement density was towards the south-east.)

Imagine my delight on discovering a washing place directly below the settlement, created by placing a boom across the East Wedderburn river. The architecture survives intact. I think about drinking the water – I want to celebrate – but for some reason, decide not to. Minutes later, I find a sheep's head in the next pool upstream. Then I realise I am using full stops for the first time in my notebook – something inside me looking for a terminus. I could wander around for ever with a mental divining-stick, but the evidence of place can only take me so far back in time, an imagined time. When does the flow of time find a direction? The Grimspound notebook consists of lineated diary entries in verse that have all been completely rewritten. As I walk back from Berry Pound, the weather changes, stray drops of rain falling on the paper. I write with a roller-ball, the ink is soon blotted, and I close the book. Uphill and downhill through a tunnel of rain everything I write dilutes and dissolves.

THE CLIMAX of Arthur Conan Doyle's *The Hound of the Baskervilles* is set in Grimspound. This is not the moment in which the villain is identified by Holmes or Watson, or the scene in which they first encounter the gigantic hound. Both these events are gripping and are triumphs of detective-story plotting. But the scene in which the hermeneutic tension of the book is brought to its most critical intensity is the one that deals with Watson's discovery of the lair of the mysterious 'man on the tor', the unknown stranger whose connection with the baffling series of events unfolding on Dartmoor is as certain as it is unfathomable. The lair is in fact one of the hut circles in the prehistoric compound. Watson discovers it after following the young boy who is supplying the 'secret man' with food and information:

> The boy was nowhere to be seen. But down beneath me in a cleft of the hills there was a circle of the old stone huts, and in the middle of them there was one which retained sufficient roof to act as a screen against the weather. My heart leaped within me as I saw it. This must be the burrow where the stranger lurked. At last my foot was on the threshold of his hiding-place – his secret was within my grasp.
>
> As I approached the hut, walking as warily as Stapleton would do when with poised net he drew near the settled butterfly, I satisfied myself that the place had indeed been used as a habitation. A vague pathway among the boulders

led to the dilapidated opening which served as a door. All was silent within. The unknown might be lurking there, or he might be prowling on the moor. My nerves tingled with the sense of adventure. Throwing aside my cigarette, I closed my hand upon the butt of my revolver, and, walking swiftly up to the door, I looked in. The place was empty.

But there were ample signs that I had not come upon a false scent. This was certainly where the man lived. Some blankets rolled in a waterproof lay upon that very stone slab upon which Neolithic man had once slumbered. The ashes of a fire were heaped in a rude grate. Beside it lay some cooking utensils and a bucket half-full of water. A litter of empty tins showed that the place had been occupied for some time, and I saw, as my eyes became accustomed to the chequered light, a pannikin and half-full bottle of spirits standing in the corner. In the middle of the hut a flat stone served the purpose of a table, and upon this stood a small cloth bundle – the same, no doubt, which I had seen through the telescope upon the shoulder of the boy. It contained a loaf of bread, a tinned tongue, and two tins of preserved peaches.[1]

Watson is expecting to encounter a kind of savage, someone or something barely human, in this prehistoric jumble of stones he thinks of as the 'burrow' of an animal. What he discovers instead is a half-full bottle of spirits and a small stock of bread and tinned goods. It is the tinned tongue that stands out, rivets our attention, speaks to us. What does it mean, to preserve a tongue, detached from its body, in a book that is full of disembodied, dislocated

---

1 Arthur Conan Doyle, *The Hound of the Baskervilles* (London: Penguin Books, 2001), pp.118–19. All subsequent references are to this edition.

voices, voices out of place, in the wrong place at the wrong time? Watson takes up his station in the hut, waiting 'with sombre patience for the coming of its tenant' (p.120), and is warned eventually of his reappearance by aural, not visual, means: first, by the 'sharp clink of a boot striking upon a stone. Then another and yet another', and finally by the sound of a voice, not the coarse voice of a brutal stranger, but the urbane, cultivated 'well-known voice' of Holmes himself. Watson's astonishment at hearing the familiar in place of the strange – it is as if the strange were ventriloquising the familiar – makes him lose hold of his own voice: 'For a moment or two I sat breathless, hardly able to believe my ears. Then my senses and my voice came back to me.'(p.121)

Voices, utterances, are unsettled, unhoused, airborne, wandering. They are most disturbing when they cannot be attached to particular bodies, precise sources:

> Again the agonized cry swept through the silent night, louder and much nearer than ever. And a new sound mingled with it, a deep, muttered rumble, musical and yet menacing, rising and falling like the low, constant murmur of the sea. (p.126)

The 'new sound' is unnerving because it seems to have no precise location, ebbing and flowing into an elemental background. Holmes attributes it to the Hound, correctly, as it turns out. But both he and Watson are incorrect in assuming that the 'agonized cry' of its victim belongs to Sir Henry Baskerville. It requires a little further detective-work to establish its owner as Selden, the escaped criminal. The cry is housed temporarily in the wrong place, just as Holmes's bivouac at Grimspound is never suspected as the habitat of Holmes himself. A prison is a holding pen for criminals but in no sense is it a home or natural habitat. The main point here is that the detective camps out in a place built originally as a settlement for people whose characters and identities have long since vanished out of all knowledge. The vocabulary of settlement has already been introduced in the description of Stapleton, the lepidopterist, approaching the 'settled butterfly', except that Stapleton is not being described directly; Watson is imagining the way the lepidopterist must operate in the process of describing his own wary movements while searching for evidence of 'habitation'. To call a butterfly 'settled' is almost to mount a contradiction in terms. And in fact, one might say that the only settled butterfly is one that has been caught, dried, mounted and framed. Conan Doyle's choice of lepidoptery as Stapleton's main pursuit enables him to place ideas about settlement and preservation at the centre of his text. If Stapleton needs to kill things in order to be able to preserve them and fix them in place, what can be said about a text that tries to fix voices in place, make them settle, in a location which is only allowed to speak of itself ventriloquially through a tin of preserved tongue?

The very first description of Grimspound in the *Hound* is provided by Stapleton:

'Prehistoric man lived thickly on the moor, and as no one in particular has lived there since, we find all his little arrangements exactly as he left them. These are his wigwams with the roofs off. You can even see his hearth and his couch if you have the curiosity to go inside.'

'But it is quite a town. When was it inhabited?'

'Neolithic man – no date.'

'What did he do?'

'He grazed his cattle on these slopes, and he learned to dig for tin when the bronze sword began to supersede the stone axe. Look at the great trench in the opposite hill. That is his mark. Yes, you will find some very singular points about the moor, Dr Watson. Oh, excuse me an instant. It is surely Cyclopides.' (p.69)

Singleton encourages us to imagine a hilltop citadel abandoned like a landlocked *Marie Celeste*, with all its 'little arrangements' left intact, which anticipates Watson's discovery of bedding, cooking utensils, and supplies. And the all-important tin of preserved tongue will be conjured up out of the grazing cattle and tin-mining that Stapleton mentions here. His choice of the term 'wigwam' makes us pause over the question of what counts as permanent settlement. How permanent is the Grimspound settlement if no one has lived in it for thousands of years? How permanent is any dwelling? During the course of the narrative, Sir Henry Baskerville returns to his ancestral home on Dartmoor, but it is the first time he has set foot anywhere near it. The Baskervilles seem like a fixture in this landscape, but Sir Henry has spent his career in Canada, just as his predecessor, Sir Charles, spent his in South Africa.

The last word of the extract, 'Cyclopides', seems to lead off on a different track, but in fact it returns us to questions of habitation. Cylopides are moth-like butterflies from South Africa, never found in England except as lepidopterists' specimens. Conan Doyle's imaginary butterfly has come to rest momentarily – or rather, is taking off from – the 'cyclopean' architecture of Grimspound. This adjective was used by Pausanias to describe the masonry of bronze age sites in Greece, especially Mycenae and Tiryns; Pliny traces its origin to Aristotle, recording a belief that the massive blocks of limestone found at these sites could only have been set in place by a race of Cyclops. When Conan Doyle first set eyes on Grimspound, in the early June of 1901, it must have struck him as a Mycenae of the north, which is exactly what it looks like today. The huge and immovable stones embedded in its gate and walls have given it a greater claim to permanence than many later structures. The circumstances of that visit in 1901 were recorded by Conan Doyle's so-called collaborator, Fletcher Robinson, in terms that reflect on the narrative choices made later in the Hound:

> From the bog, we tramped eastward to the stone fort of Grimspound, which the savages of the Stone Age in Britain... raised with enormous labour to act as a haven of refuge from the marauding tribes to the South. The good preservation in which the Grimspound fort still remains is marvellous... Into one of these [stone huts] Doyle and I walked, and sitting down on the stone which probably served the three thousand year old chief as a bed we talked of the races of the past. It was one of the loneliest spots in Great Britain... Suddenly we heard a boot strike against a stone without and rose together. It was only a lonely tourist on a walking excursion, but at the sight of our heads suddenly emerging from the hut he let out a yell and bolted... as he did not return I have small doubt Mr Doyle and I added yet another proof of the supernatural to tellers of ghost stories concerning Dartmoor.[2]

It may be that Robinson's anecdote is coloured by his reading of the Hound: the detail of the boot striking against the stone is put to telling use in Conan Doyle's narrative. But his account of the physical dispositions reverses the relative positions of advantage and disadvantage in the Hound.

---

2 November 1905, Associated Sunday Magazines, quoted in Christopher Frayling's Introduction to the Penguin edition.

Watson settles himself in the stone hut but is unsettled by the arrival of a stranger; in Robinson's version it is the other way round. Conan Doyle takes every opportunity to complicate the identifying marks of a settled state. His Sir Henry Baskerville is both a tourist, a Canadian visitor, and the scion of a family with deep roots in the vicinity. Seen from the point of view of Dr Mortimer, who collects human specimens as avidly as Stapleton collects butterflies and moths, Baskerville has all the identifying marks of an aboriginal: 'A glance at our friend here reveals the rounded head of the Celt, which carries inside it the Celtic enthusiasm and power of attachment.' (p.55)

Baskerville, the human artefact, is environed by museum specialists, experts in classification and conservation. But Mortimer is given the role of protector, while Stapleton belongs to the genre of collector as exterminator, his private museum illustrating how far he will go to achieve his own vision of order, whatever the cost to other creatures, animal or human:

> The room had been fashioned into a small museum, and the walls were lined by a number of glass-topped cases full of that collection of butterflies and moths the formation of which had been the relaxation of this complex and dangerous man. In the centre of this room there was an upright beam, which had been placed at some period as a support for the old worm-eaten balk of timber which spanned the roof. To this post a figure was tied, so swathed and muffled in sheets which had been used to secure it that one could not for the moment tell whether it was that of a man or a woman. One towel passed round the throat, and was secured at the back of the pillar. Another covered the lower part of the face and over it two dark eyes – eyes full of grief and shame and a dreadful questioning – stared back at us.

In a minute we had torn off the gag, unswathed the bonds, and Mrs Stapleton sank upon the floor in front of us. As her beautiful head fell upon her chest I saw the clear red weal of a whip-lash across her neck. (pp.151–2)

Mrs Stapleton is nothing more nor less than the prize exhibit in a collection of dead things; she is still alive, but Holmes and company are only just in time to ensure this. She is pinned to the beam like a butterfly or moth mounted in a case, but she is also 'swathed and muffled' lie an Egyptian mummy, the archetypal museum specimen of preserved human tissue, the literal embodiment of humanity's desire to avoid being 'worm-eaten'. The towel that secures her throat and the gag that is torn from her mouth draw attention to the silencing of her voice, and place her mummified appearance in a category of objects that evoke the suspension of voice whose epitome is the tin of preserved tongue.

In one sense, Stapleton's need to paralyse the living, making still what is quick and restless, joins with Watson's anxiety that whatever is stirring on the moor does not belong there; or, to be more precise, it is something belonging to that place that does not belong to that time – something alive that ought to be dead: 'If you were to see a skin-clad, hairy man crawl out from the low door, fitting a flint-tipped arrow on to the string of his bow, you would feel that his presence there was more natural than your own' (p.75). Watson's vocabulary suggests that the 'natural' state of humanity might be one of primitive aggression: survival through competition of a kind that pre-dates the establishment of law and order. His imagination populates the hut circles alternately with examples of prehistoric man and the modern convict. He writes to Holmes that the ancient compound is most likely where the escaped convict has gone to earth: 'Of course so far as his concealment goes there is no difficulty

at all. Any one of these huts would give him a hiding-place'
(p.76). But the convict himself seems to exist in two dif-
ferent time-frames: as the adult murderer, and as his own
childhood self, which is how his sister continues to think of
him, despite the criminal career overlying and obliterating
the juvenile version: 'To all the world he was the man of
violence, half animal and half demon; but to her he always
remained the little wilful boy of her own girlhood, the child
who had clung to her hand' (p.135). If early man is associat-
ed with the threat of violence, the early history of the self
seems to hinge on vulnerability, on the need for protection.
When Watson thinks he is on the convict's trail, he is actu-
ally following a boy, the boy who brings the tinned tongue
and bottled spirits to the hut circle. Except that this boy is
not 'wilful' – he acts according to the will of Holmes.

Selden's appearance in death only strengthens the link
that Watson has made already between the convict and the
prehistory of the site: his face 'might well have belonged to
one of those old savages who dwelt in the burrows on the
hillside' (p.96), while Stapleton, who conceals his Bask-
erville heredity, is unmasked when Holmes compares his
physiognomy with that of the Baskerville family portraits:
'it is an interesting case of a throwback, which appears to
be both physical and spiritual. A study of family portraits
is enough to convert a man to the doctrine of reincarna-
tion' (p.138). In this context, the subject matter of Mor-
timer's three published papers, mentioned early on in the
story – 'Is Disease a Reversion?', 'Some Freaks of Atavism'
and 'Do We Progress?'(p.8) – echoes the text's own obses-
sion with the collapsing of time-frames. Doyle's own sto-
ry is driven by the fascination for the reader of repeated
narrative patterns; of the possibility that the sequence of
actions recorded in the Baskerville family legend will recur
time and time again. The legend reaches its climax with

the spectacle of the giant hound standing over Sir Hugo
Baskerville and 'plucking at his throat' (p.15); the Sherlock
Holmes story leads to the same point: 'I was in time to see
the beast spring upon its victim, hurl him to the ground
and worry at his throat'(p.149). Up until now, the hound
has been heard but not seen, with its 'muttered rumble'
seemingly dislocated from its source in the animal's throat.
Both in the legend and in Watson's case history, the imme-
diate object of the hound's attack is the victim's throat and
the root of the tongue; which is where the voice originates;
where language is housed. The case history is a species of
'throwback' in language, while the language of the legend
proves to be premonitory.

But it is the setting of both legend and case history that
ensures the collapsing of time-frames: a setting in which
the nature of the landscape provides a crucial element
in the detective-story plot, while slowing down the rate
of change so much that repeated actions seem almost to
co-exist in a region of temporal stasis. It is the peat bog
setting that preserves physical matter even while it swal-
lows up moorland ponies and specimens of humanity. The
peat holds objects from the past destined to become future
exhibits, or the stuff of future memories. Watson refers at
one point to 'touching bottom' as a guarantee or criteri-
on of certainty: 'It is something to have touched bottom
anywhere in this bog in which we are floundering'. (p.88)
But touching bottom in a peat bog is a guarantee only of
extinction. Stapleton alone had 'learned to penetrate the
Grimpen Mire' (p.158) but despite his being able to nav-
igate his way through the quagmire, Stapleton is sucked
down into it and penetrated by its mixture of water and or-
ganic materials. The text itself anticipates the slow decom-
position of Baskerville bodies at the very moment of Sir
Henry's arrival on the scene: 'The rattle of our wheels died

away as we drove through drifts of rotting vegetation – sad gifts, as it seemed to me, for Nature to throw before the carriage of the returning heir of the Baskervilles.' (p.56)

In one way or another, the figures who populate the story and its setting are imagined as the forerunners of their own afterlives. When Mortimer, the cranial enthusiast, first encounters Holmes, he sees him primarily as a skullcarrier – as a future exhibit in an anthropological museum – while he himself is described in terms that render him a candidate for inclusion in Stapleton's entomological collection: 'He had long, quivering fingers as agile and restless as the antennae of an insect'(p.10). Mortimer is most alive when handling the relics of the dead: 'He has been excavating a barrow at Long Down, and has got a prehistoric skull which fills him with great joy' (p.78). He enters the story in order to disclose the document that provides its essential narrative kernel, the Baskerville legend, and reads it aloud in a 'high, crackling voice' that resembles the sound of a primitive recording mechanism. Two years before writing the Hound, Conan Doyle had published 'The Story of the Japanned Box', which centres on the 'strange, crisp, metallic clicking' of a phonograph that preserves the last words of a dying woman, whose entreaty to her husband is projected into the future. The manuscript of the Baskerville legend draws attention to its own afterlife in the hands of its readers: 'Learn then from this story not to fear the fruits of the past, but rather to be circumspect in the future' (p.13). Stapleton, under his assumed name of Vandeleur, is credited with the discovery of a particular moth species, so that his own change of identity is attached to the life cycle of a creature undergoing metamorphosis. His collection of lepidoptera is assembled in the same building where he runs his school, for young humans at a larval stage of development whose minds he intends to mould, 'impressing them with one's own character and ideals' (p.72), so that they too become part of a collection whose primary aim is to reflect the ambition of the collector.

Conan Doyle arranges the narrative so that Holmes and Watson gravitate towards Stapleton as chief suspect, and they are described as doing so like a pair of lepidopterists closing in on a 'settled butterfly'. Once he has assembled most of the evidence he needs, Homes produces the vocabulary of the collector: 'My nets are closing upon him, even as his are upon Sir Henry' (p.126). There might seem to be a natural justice in this lexical symmetry, although the avidity with which the detective looks forward to closing the file on Stapleton is somewhat disconcerting: 'We have him, Watson, we have him, and I dare swear that before tomorrow night he will be fluttering in our net as helpless as one of his own butterflies. A pin, a cork, and a card, and we add him to the Baker Street collection!'(p.138) Whether Holmes derives more relish from the capture of his prey, or from its extinction, is difficult to say. But the 'Baker Street collection' is not, of course, a chamber of horrors, but a series of casebooks, and the primary objective of the investigative procedure in any given case is not to establish the legal or moral case for nailing the villain, but to complete the narrative pattern.

The case-history is a *summa* of deductions, providing a reconstruction of the acts and circumstances that lie behind a specific crime, but the investigations of Holmes and Watson sponsor a discursive investigation into the prehistory of the place where that crime is committed, and the prehistory of its agents and patients. Holmes sounds the keynote on the very first page of the text, asking Watson to deduce the prehistory of the stick that Mortimer has left in their Baker Street flat: 'this accidental souvenir becomes of importance. Let me hear you reconstruct the man by an examination of it' (p.5). Watson provides an outline that Holmes corrects and extends. Like a pair of archaeologists, they reconstruct the culture to which the object belongs, showing how the artefact itself possesses a kind of memory; how its reflection of the milieu from which it has sprung is inevitable. As the souvenir of a specific history, it is anything but accidental.

The text begins with a model example of the technique and theme of reconstruction. Holmes provides the example, which the narrator, Watson, relates. The latter states that his chief objective is to 'give publicity' (p.6) to Holmes's methods, which adds another layer of reconstruction to the process. And what he proceeds to recount are precisely his memories of looking forward to Holmes's own reconstructions of past events: 'I feel that it is best that I should let you have all the facts and leave you to select for yourself those which will be of most service to you in helping you to your conclusions' (p.98).

Both Holmes and Watson note the decisive role of balancing 'alternative theories' (p.27) and balancing 'probabilities' (p.35) in pursuit of a conclusion, and the decisive factor in reaching a conclusion is the achievement of form, the allure of coherence: 'The thing takes shape, Watson. It becomes coherent' (p.30). The allure of the detective story plot is the harmony it gives to seemingly discordant elements; the underlying pattern that Watson gives voice to. The language of reconstruction is what loosens the story's tongue. But reconstruction gives only one version; and is the result of choosing between alternatives. In some respects, it is a kind of translation, from one language to another, and its relation to its own prehistory is like that of a living organ to a tin of preserved tongue. The morphology is the same; the experience radically different.

The text of The Hound of the Baskervilles includes an

emblem of its own status as a container for things that have been re-composed in the message left for Sir Henry Baskerville at the Northumberland Hotel. The message consists of printed letters cut out of a copy of *The Times* and pasted onto a foolscap sheet. Holmes ascertains that the letters have been excised from an article on Free Trade – an economic principle that encourages the free movement of goods between different societies and cultures. The letters have been combined into a message that warns against movement between locations: 'As you value your life or your reason keep away from the moor'(p.32). Movement towards the moor entails movement towards Sir Henry's ancestral home and heredity, as well as towards the pre-history of the crucial location: the site of Grimspound. It entails movement in time as well as space.

When Watson first makes the move to Baskerville Hall, he notes the ruins of the old Lodge and the incomplete condition of its replacement 'a new building, half constructed' (p.58) representing the abandonment of those 'schemes of reconstruction and improvement'(p.16) interrupted by the death of Sir Charles. When his heir, Sir Henry, arrives on the scene, it is evident that 'our friend has large ideas, and means to spare no pains or expense to restore the grandeur of his family. When the house is renovated and refurnished, all that he will need will be a wife to make it complete' (pp.83–4). This compulsion to renovate and reconstruct arises from an obscure need to restore what has been lost; which, in both cases, is a sense of connection with the place. But it might also reflect Conan Doyle's fascination with the reconstructive mania of Sabine Baring-Gould, the Victorian excavator of Grimspound.

3

GRIMSPOUND WAS DUG over a period of two and a half weeks in 1894, by a team of local workmen supervised by a team of local worthies: the Reverend Sabine Baring-Gould, Mr Robert Burnard, Mr R.N. Worth, Mr R. Hansford Worth, the Reverend W.A.G. Gray and one Dr Prowse. All but Prowse signed the excavation report drafted by Baring-Gould and published in July in the *Report and Transactions of the Devonshire Association*, Vol.XXVI. There is no doubt that Baring-Gould and Burnard were the two heavyweights in this enterprise; and their views on archaeological method did not quite join up. Burnard was the founding Secretary of the Dartmoor Preservation Association whose mission was the 'protection and preservation' of the status quo on Dartmoor; Baring-Gould was a best-selling historical novelist whose experiments in archaeology, architecture and musicology were driven by a desire to re-fashion whatever survived of the past in line with his own predilections. And he was accustomed to getting his own way. In 1849, aged fifteen, he had discovered a Roman villa at Pau in the south of France. With no formal training in archaeology, he directed a team of French workmen and uncovered a mosaic pavement, reputedly two hundred feet long. Apparently, he took careful notes and made watercolour drawings of his findings, but the pavement itself was left to disintegrate.

Although he was heir of the Lewtrenchard estate on Dartmoor, he did not take up his inheritance until 1881, at the age of forty-seven. And before that date his life was profoundly unsettled. His eccentric father opted for an itinerant life, travelling round Europe by coach with his entire family in tow. As a result, the young Sabine spent less than three years in England, between the ages of three and sixteen, although when he returned to England for good, he possessed an eclectic knowledge of several European cultures and spoke five languages. He studied at Cambridge, where he was known for his piety, defied his father's plan that he should teach at Marlborough and went instead to Pimlico to teach slum children. Two other teaching posts followed before he took up orders; then he went to a curacy in Yorkshire, which he loved, and a rectorship in East Mersea, which he loathed – all the time keeping up a manic rate of literary production.

When he installed himself at Lewtrenchard as squarson (= squire + parson) his condition was that of the Return of the Native. His family history meant he belonged to Devon, but his formative experiences lay elsewhere. He saw the west of England in relation to long and broad historical perspectives; and regarded Dartmoor as the site of encounters between natives and incomers – as a crucible for intermixing different racial stocks. Baring-Gould's Presidential Address to the July 1896 meeting of the Devonshire Association embodies the outlook of a man for whom a sustained exposure to different national characters had produced a mindset of profound atavism. In this lengthy policy document, he identifies the invasion of Aryan 'swarms' into Europe during the Neolithic period with the arrival of a new, brachycephalic, type of skull. The resulting fusion of dolichocephalic and brachycephalic skull-types did not coincide with the cultural domination of the former by the latter, but rather the opposite:

> But if the Goidel invaders subjugated the Ivernians, they were in their turn conquered by them, though in a different manner. The strongly-marked religious ideas of the

long-headed men, and their deeply-rooted habit of wor-
ship of ancestors, impressed and captured the imagination
of their masters, and as the races became fused, the mixed
race continued to build dolmens and erect other megalith-
ic monuments once characteristic of the long-heads, often
on a larger scale than before.[3]

Exactly like Dr Mortimer in The Hound of the Baskervilles,
Baring-Gould is obsessed with craniology, not simply as a
means of reconstructing the prehistory of Dartmoor from
the evidence of human remains, but as a basis for deter-
mining the survival of archaic traits within the present day
population:

We are hindered in making great way by the absence of
skulls and skeletons of prehistoric man in our barrows on
the granite and the clay. Nor can we expect to find them.
But the present inhabitants of the county are with us, and
perhaps not altogether indisposed to be observed and com-
mented upon. They are lineal descendants of the men who
set up the rude stone monuments, and tomahawked each
other, first with stone axes, and then with bronze celts…

In conclusion, I would urge on the Devon Association
the importance of collecting statistics relative to the shape
of heads, the colour of eyes and hair, and complexion of
the children in our schools.[4]

3 Rev.S.Baring-Gould, 'President's Address', Report and
Transactions of the Devonshire Association for the Advancement of Science,
Literature, and Art [South Molton, July, 1894] (Plymouth: William
Brendon and Son, 1894) pp.38–9.
4 Ibid, p.47.

The urgency of this call to action is heightened by the influence of the railways in 'distributing our population and breaking up the little clusters of families that have remained in one district for centuries'.[5] It is precisely by means of the railway system that Sherlock Holmes distributes himself; or rather, the efficiency of the railway creates the illusion of his being in two different places at once: in London, at the heart of modernity; and on the moor, in pursuit of the human 'throwback'. The railway is the enemy of ethnography, but it modernises the system of criminal investigation.

Mortimer notes that Sir Henry Baskerville has the 'rounded head' of a Celt – he is both the heir of the estate and an *arriviste*, having spent his career in Canada. His condition recalls that of the second wave of invaders, outwardly in control, but inwardly succumbing to the traditions of the place they come to own. His uncle fits the same pattern, having made his fortune in South Africa. Both men seek to renew the building projects of their forerunners, unconsciously echoing the practices of Baring-Gould's 'short-headed' invaders who extended the tradition of dolmen-building established by the 'long-headed Ivernians.' But the Baskerville improvers also echo the practices of Sabine Baring-Gould himself, who personally relocated the Lewtrenchard 'menhir', or standing stone, which had been used time out of mind as a bridge over the millstream. Baring-Gould had it dragged to the front of the mill and re-erected.

This simple act of restoration was the small tip of a large floe of renovation schemes. Two years before Sabine's birth in 1834, his uncle Charles had remodelled Lewtrenchard church. All the medieval oak pews and the rood-screen were removed and replaced with deal box-pews, in keeping

---

5 Ibid, pp.47–8.

with early nineteenth-century taste. Seventeen years later when the boy was fifteen, he visited the family home and unearthed the remains of the old woodwork. At once he made himself a promise to restore the church, and hid the medieval carpentry where no one would find it. When he returned thirty-two years later, he reconstructed the rood screen, using the old fragments and a water colour drawing of the original arrangements. Local craftsmen were employed to produce this replica, which took twenty-six years to complete. Original works were also introduced into the scheme, and the church gradually filled up with an eclectic range of paintings, stained glass windows, lecterns, chandeliers and a great brass cross; all collected during Baring-Gould's sorties across Europe. There were artefacts from Munich, Switzerland, Brittany and Belgium. The ensemble did not reflect the cultural history of a Devonshire church but the eccentric career of a dilettante.

Much the same was true of Lewtrenchard House, which underwent a complete transformation. The exterior was refaced with local stone; the interior remodelled according to Baring-Gould's own design – he never engaged an architect for any of his building schemes. He introduced a projecting porch and built a library and a ballroom projecting at either end of the old hall, to produce the effect of an E-shaped Elizabethan house. It was a complete pastiche, and even incorporated a '1620' date stone into the new work over the main entrance. The stone had been taken from another building altogether. Yet when the makeover was finished, Baring-Gould reputedly exclaimed, 'It is lovely to be living at last in a genuine seventeenth-century house.'[6]

6 Bickford H.C.Dickinson, *Sabine Baring-Gould: Squarson, Writer and Folklorist, 1834–1924* (Newton Abbot: David & Charles, 1970), p.107.

He indulged himself, yet earned a good reputation as both squire and rector. But he must have made frequent use of curates, given the amount of time he spent outside the parish. He was for many years the key figure in the Dartmoor Exploration Committee, and led many of its expeditions. The Grimspound excavation report was its first publication. And from 1890 onwards he was also heavily engaged in collecting the folk songs of Devon and Cornwall. The huge corpus of songs he amassed was later edited by Cecil Sharp, and Sharp's reputation as a musicologist has certainly eclipsed that of his predecessors. But there is no doubt that Baring-Gould was responsible for the legwork, for jogging the memories of his aging and ailing informants (some of whom were bedridden and crack-voiced) and for recording their words.

But he was also tempted to change their words − and gave into temptation enough times to obscure the very unblurry line between what came out of the communal voice of popular culture and what came out of the mind of the cleric. His day job was the moral and spiritual instruction of his flock; and so he bowdlerised the songs of the West. Torn between preserving the authentic imprint of cultural memory and his own aversion to profanity, he suppressed everything that was obscene in content and toned down what was coarse in expression. The effect was acquiescent in the prudishness of the times, but it was also a bid to keep in circulation as much as possible of the sound and feel of a disappearing world. Baring-Gould's folk song project turned out to be a very successful failure: it publicised the legacy of the 'song men' (and a couple of women) of the western counties; but only in his edited version. Plymouth Library holds a copy of the songs exactly as they were transcribed, and in some cases, the final versions are totally different. The corpus was published − with the specious subtitle 'a collection made from the mouths of the people' – in 1892, two years before the expedition to Grimspound.

Baring-Gould led the attack on Grimspound with his own reconstruction programme at Lewtrenchard under way, and his rehabilitation of the folksong project in the bag. He arrived fully prepared to edit, revise, repair and reimagine anything that stood in his way. He had already appointed George French as foreman, having worked with him before at Broadun Ring, another Bronze Age settlement site. French had recommended himself by displaying an enthusiasm 'not surpassed by that of any of the members of the committee', but his real value to Baring-Gould was his 'long experience in wall-building'. This, and his 'general practical knowledge, rendered his judgment in disputed matters of the highest consequence'.[7] The conjunction of 'disputed matters' and 'wall-building' shows that there was opposition to the idea of restoring the ruined hut circles, although one of the larger huts, number three, was comprehensively restored. Lesley Chapman mentions in his guide to 'The Ancient Dwellings of Grimspound and Hound Tor' that the Dartmoor Exploration Committee also 'repaired or rebuilt part of the enclosure wall' and that 'there were some members of the Committee who disapproved of the rebuilding'(Crediton: Orchard Publications, 1996). In his report Baring-Gould edits out all signs of disquiet or disagreement, and even presents the restoration process as an expression of shared purpose:

---

7 'The Exploration of Grimspound: First Report of the Dartmoor Exploration Committee', *Report and Transactions of the Devonshire Association for the Advancement of Science, Literature, and Art* Vol.XXVI (Plymouth: William Brendon and Son, 1894), p.102.

Owing to the remarkable condition of preservation in which this hut was, the Committee resolved to re-construct the walls where fallen, to bank them up with turf, and then to enclose the whole with iron hurdles; and to leave the floor exposed, with hearth, dais, and cooking hole, for the enlightenment of visitors interested in the pre-historic antiquities of Dartmoor.[8]

One such visitor, only seven years later, was Conan Doyle, whose imagination had no difficulty populating this stage-set with the *dramatis personae* of his work-in-progress. But there are signs that Baring-Gould was bothered by the resistance offered by some members of the committee, in his repeating the same point about the system used to displace certain of the wall stones of Grimspound, but not others:

> The turf was taken off from the entire surface within the ring, then the 'meat earth' was removed, and such stones as had fallen in were by this means exposed. Such stones, when loose and small, were thereupon placed on the walls, but all such as seemed earth-fast were left untouched.[9]

The Committee have been most careful not to destroy anything during the investigations. No earthfast stone has been consciously moved; only such fallen stones as were obviously out of place have been removed from the soil they covered; and the floors of the huts cleared of the accumulations of rubbish that lay on them... When the grass springs again, Grimspound will be as it was, excepting only that it has yielded up some of its secrets, and that it can be looked upon with an intelligent understanding of its

---

8 Ibid, p.109.
9 Ibid, p.105.

purpose and the cultural stage to which it belonged, and no longer with vague wonder.[10]

Sheltering behind 'the Committee', Baring-Gould validates the repositioning of fallen stones – under the licence provided by the mere presence of George French, with his wall-building expertise – but the insistence that no 'earthfast' stone has been *consciously* moved is a refinement on the initial assertion that any stone fixed in the ground was left in place, and reads like the stirring of a guilty awareness that no system is foolproof. Moreover, Baring-Gould recruits 'intelligent understanding' in the service of reconstruction, mocking the 'vague wonder' of responses to the site before investigation. He also takes the unusual step of specifying how many committee members were present to supervise the workmen:

> A further decision was arrived at that, whenever possible, two members at least should be present each day during the investigation… On three days only during the course of the explorations was a single member in charge, on six there were two to watch the proceedings, on six days there were three, and on one day five. On a single day only were the workmen engaged without a member of the committee being present to supervise…[11]

Out of a total of seventeen days, there were seven when supervision was satisfactory, six when it was no more than adequate, three when it was badly lacking, and one when it was totally lacking. The roll-call is not as reassuring as Baring-Gould would like it to be. Without proper

---

10 Ibid, p.119.
11 Ibid, p.102.

supervision, the local labour would have reverted to un-conscious habits of drystone building with the best material to hand, using stones that were the right size and shape; tempted perhaps by 'earth-fast' stones that seemed loose enough to them.

As supervisor-in-chief, Baring-Gould had his own 'wonder' issues. The scale of Grimspound was enough to sponsor an imaginative reconstruction of the site that made it the pivot of the region and the epitome of a social and cultural revolution that would extend over a continent:

> When, moreover, we consider that the circumference of the wall measures over 1,500 feet, it becomes obvious that such an extent presupposes some two hundred defenders. Presumably, Grimspound was not a fortified village, any more than it was merely a cattle pound, but was the *oppidum*, the place of refuge for the scattered population on Hookner and Hameldon, and the twelve householders within the enclosure were the *oppidani*, the guardians in time of peace. This was, as we know, the system among the Gauls, and the Gallic men of Iron who invaded the land now called France, almost certainly adopted this system from the Neolithic and Bronze race which they overcame, and whose land they occupied, and whose rites and super-stitions they adopted.[12]

Baring-Gould adds one speculation to another; trans-forming a pound for stock animals into the last redoubt of a people whose social structure is conjured up out of Roman campaign reports written down a millennium later, with the anomaly removed by his own theory of cultural assimilation. His imaginative re-enactment of the

12 Ibid, pp.114–15.

Grimspounders' last stand is the default mode of the historical novelist. By contrast, Robert Burnard's report of the excavation he directed at Broadun and Broadun Ring over three weeks in August and September 1893 is a model of scientific restraint. In point of fact, the circumference of the wall at Broadun is greater than that of Grimspound, which casts a shadow over Baring-Gould's daydream about Grimspound being the regional *oppidum*. Burnard's approach is to describe and measure every feature of every hut circle; to list the inorganic materials used, and to analyse the organic materials (for example, to determine the exact type of wood charcoal found in any given hearth). Artefacts, such as worked flints, are carefully assessed. The record is meticulous and exhaustive. There is no speculation; no hypotheses about the inhabitants' cultural identity or customs. The only comparative observation refers to a contemporary anthropological account of the cooking practices of the Assineboin people of North America, because like the Bronze Age inhabitants of Dartmoor, they too use cooking stones in cooking pits filled with water, rather than cooking vessels on open fires. And this single departure from what is otherwise an exhaustive inventory of finds, is only there to shed light on the total absence from both sites of even the smallest fragment of pottery.

One page into his report, Burnard discloses that 'in my digging operations, I was accompanied for the most part by the Rev. S. Baring-Gould',[13] but there is no doubt that Burnard owned this operation and the way it was conducted. Their attitudes and objectives, their styles and methods,

---

13 Robert Burnard, 'Exploration of the Hut Circles in Broadun Ring and Broadun', *Report and Transactions of the Devonshire Association for the Advancement of Science, Literature and Art*,Vol.XXVI, (Plymouth: William Brendon and Son, 1894), p.187.

could not have been more different. Though opposite in many ways, both were natural candidates for leadership of the Dartmoor Exploration Committee. It seems most likely that Burnard would have been first to disapprove of Baring-Gould's appetite for rebuilding parts of Grimspound. We do not know how this rivalry played out in the dynamic of the Committee and its various expeditions. In their reports, there is no indication of a power struggle, but it would have been bad publicity to reveal any evidence of discord in a society that brought recognition and respect to all concerned.

It was a different matter when someone else was authoring the report. Nearly twenty years after the initial excavation, Grimspound was made the highlight of the transactions of the Devonshire Association. After three and a half days of scholarly papers, public speeches and Council business, the fifty second annual meeting of the Association was rounded off with a visit to the site. Members of the Royal Archaeological Institute of Great Britain and Ireland had arranged to meet them there, to hear in situ a paper on the excavation. This was a big moment for Devon's finest, when they could show off their best practice and gain national recognition. Naturally, Sabine Baring-Gould was asked to do the honours. He accepted, but on the actual day, Friday 25 July 1913, was 'prevented' from doing so 'owing to an unfortunate accident'. What species of accident this was, is unclear, but it did not prevent him from attending – he was 'well enough to be present at this historic gathering'. He must have known that his place would be taken by Robert Burnard – and it was.

Perhaps Baring-Gould had taken stock of what purpose this visit served for the Royal Archaeological Institute. They were there to check up. Before the local man was given a chance to open his mouth, the President of the Institute, Sir Henry Howorth, read the Riot Act. His delegation did not visit the provinces for their own amusement, but to bring the provincial societies into line with national standards of excavation. He admitted that 'methods of archaeological research had improved' in Devon since his own last visit to the county – which was a relief: for 'there is nothing more wicked in the world, than the destruction of antiquities by antiquaries'. He then emphasised that 'a great many churches had been utterly desolated by methods of what was called restoration'. This might have been aimed directly at Baring-Gould, in which case, the charge of wickedness would have stung the rector in him. Howorth then drew a parallel between church restoration and certain styles of archaeological excavation: 'it was similar in the case of prehistoric monuments, where in many cases, people would dig in a most extraordinarily stupid way… What they now wanted was that the work of every cubic yard should be carefully mapped out.' Cue Robert Burnard. Howorth's ultimatum was a direct challenge to those thinking of excavating a site such as Grimspound:

'Let me implore you,' he concluded, 'whatever plea you get for digging the site of a mound or any monument of primitive times, put an absolute embargo upon it unless the man in charge is a scientific man who understands scientific digging.'[14]

---

14 Maxwell Adams, 'Proceedings at the Fifty-Second Annual Meeting held at Buckfastleigh, 22–25 July, 2013', *Report and Transactions of the Devonshire Association for the Advancement of Science, Literature, and Art*', Vol. XLV (Plymouth: William Brendon and Son, 1913), p.36.

Burnard then stepped forward and coolly gave everyone an object lesson in precise and thorough description, before offering some conclusions that cancelled out Baring-Gould's vision of Grimspound as the beating heart of an entire region – the sacred precinct of the guardians of the race. This was a summary dismissal of his colleague's most cherished theory:

> As in the case of the majority of Dartmoor 'circles', it could not be said that the finds and the state of the original floors of the huts gave any indication that they were occupied for any lengthened period. This confirmed the theory that Grimspound was never finished, and that the intention – if it ever existed – of making the place a kind of protected village, instead of a mere animal fold, was never completely carried out.[15]

As soon as this demolition order had been handed out to Baring-Gould's dream construction, which had made a kind of Bronze Age Camelot out of an animal fold, Howorth stepped forward and heaped praise on its author, acclaiming Burnard's paper as a 'masterpiece for the amount of information it contained in a brief space, and its clarity'. Burnard carried himself with a professional restraint at all times and presumably would not have made a show of his pleasure at this public recognition of his qualities. But Baring-Gould must have been in a state of tumult.

And worse was to come. Howorth then turned aside to acknowledge his presence among them, an unexpected pleasure given the 'unfortunate accident' that prevented them from hearing a paper by him. The President of the Royal Archaeological Institute then paid him the savagely

---

15 Ibid, p.38.

back-handed compliment of being 'one of the most fertile and picturesque antiquaries in the realm'. In other words: we recognise Baring-Gould as part of the problem: that of 'the destruction of antiquities by antiquaries'. He has an overactive imagination, and his concrete actions are governed by a desire to enhance the aesthetic dimension of the 'visitor experience' — as in the rebuilding of hut three for the 'enlightenment of visitors'; or the rebuilding of his own home to arrive at a feeling of what it was like to live in a 'genuine' seventeenth-century house. The Rector of Lewtrenchard must have seen his life flash before his eyes at this point. And it was true that much of it, from the age of fifteen at least, had been spent in pursuit of his own dreams — some of which took fictional form while others had been material interventions in actual sites and buildings.

The past itself was hidden behind versions, some scientific, some not. Baring-Gould knew that the most compelling versions fired the imagination, and that history would give way to legend, when the time was right. The time was the last long hot summer before the Great War, when his race theories were soon to break surface in the present, like an ancient organism spewed out by a peat bog. When the organism formed the basis of a superstition — like that of the Hound of the Baskervilles — careful, scientific reconstruction could expose it as a sham; but when it let slip the dogs of war, it played havoc with the real, and groaned for burial.

4

the new leaf climbs the air
the bee tickles the plant
and the wolf has suckled its young

the swallows gather
to make their magic
and lose the memory
of the dark hours

we cook with the stones
taken from the river
where beavers destroyed the net
and brought bad luck

*

now the clan is inside the self
like the tooth of a boar

but father drives away the
uncle with broken leg-bone

and evil mouth the one
who yawns and groans
when his thigh wound swells
who sucks on the necks of the weak

dragging the child towards the fire
to make his guts jump

pain is wedged in his soul

he is not the owner of his revenge

*

father feels the flash in the loins
and the spurt of denial

he is still the best hunter

bowstring at his throat
he can see the eyelash of marten quiver

he creeps like a spy to chop off the tail
of a snake heavy with young

*

the embryo becomes visible

then is pushed away
and set free to cover
and bind with a pelt

the belly now loose as dust

the first strong lock of hair
is given with outstretched hand
and burned with a feather

the father spends these nights in the open

he is watching all the dead stars
   being swept out of heaven

*

I could hardly breathe watching
the mountain deer stand still

even the sparrows were quiet
for a smell we could not recognise

a dove burning in the air

*

there is light on the horizon
like a dorsal fin

but the daybreak is weak

now ashes fall like snow
from the limits of the world

and the rain seethes
where it touches the earth

*

we stumble upon the smell of smoke
the sharp reek of sacrifice

men pile up charcoal in the pit
and fashion prayers

to peel the shadow from the sun

to free the mist from the moon

they smear the marrow
on breast and chin
elbow bent and ready

to rake the flesh

*

there is a great flapping of wings
in the enclosure

the crows have grasped a kid

and a jackal waits by the big tree
its belly stiff with hunger

father must shoulder the goat
and take it to the hollow bank

where the women carve the chalk
and bend the clay

I must keep watch on the foal

*

father is shaking mad
he is heavy with care

his brother's stealth was like

a stab in the palm of the hand
a blow on the back of the neck

the loss kneads his heart
they were born from the same womb
they set out on the same path

now he must follow the tracks
into the lowlands

knowing they are too faint

*

a rider has come
for many days on horseback

he dismounts with a heavy stagger

he speaks of a deep gulf

a gorge with a river far below
a tiny moving glitter

everywhere else there is drought

we have made our circle of wall
and a pitfall for antelopes

we have imprisoned the stream

*

my sister gathers pot-herb and sorrel

while I stoop and muck out the stalls
make perches for house-birds

*

the rider sleeps in the store-house
his horse is isabel-yellow

in the middle of the night
I dream of his long staff
resting on the flesh of his thigh

when he asks me a riddle
I search for the right answer

but he rolls aside to my sister
I see his hand on the groove of her back

I stretch and scrape at the thatch
to let in more light

but his hand moves on to a new place
where the skin is as smooth as butter

*

sister says   there is a new light in heaven
to gird around the waist of the earth

but when I looked out   from under the dripstone
through the drizzle
        I saw only a steep bank of cloud
running away

and the last embers of the sun
        blaze up

*

father went out to check the snares
        in the evening glow
said he had seen a stranger beckoning

but when he went near
        it looked like the face
had been gnawed away

it made him giddy
        it made him sink down
as if on the edge of an abyss

he could not sleep
        until break of day

in case it was the ancestor
        the spinner of dreams
come to make an end of him

*

I put on my kerchief
step into the deep snow
and poke the ground

in search of the year-old sheep

the one whose navel-string
I had to bite

I wear a dogskin pouch on my back
hands free to clamber
                and make my way
to the standpoint on the hill

but someone or something is there on the crag
quite still
            as if ready to spring away

it makes me think of my uncle

some say a great bird
once seized his ankle

and cut the leg-root
                for bearing tales

others say it was not a bird
but a spirit
            a great one
the lord of a distant time

when the land was covered in waves
with nowhere under the vault of the sky
                        for birds to settle
and nowhere for swimmers to rise to the shore

until the great ones
put the world in order

                    leaving a footprint
on the shore

that is now the great rock-sanctuary upstream
where birds do settle and remain
                    leaving a lure
in the waves
a feather from the quiver
                        of the fisher-god
who has the right to lure a bride
                            into the sea
and put his arm around her

or draw her into the great mire
to be sucked in and swallowed

                            *

there is a saying
                that those without land
are left with nothing but the scabs on their wounds

it is silent over the hill
where everyone has gone

first there was fever   and a strange lightness
then a swelling jaw
                and a tetter all over the body
then every living thing died out

sometimes we heard them wail
                when the wind was in the east

                            *

in the pit was one of twins
                on a pointed stake

father ran out with a knobbed club
                    to tear his brother asunder

he found him with the lamb tied to a tree
and a boast in his windpipe

in the palm of his hand
                a lock of human hair
and the smell of wood-tar

*

father says we must draw lots for the gods
to let them come
                on this side of the world

he says I have the gift

I know how to draw lines
                on the hearth stone
and scour the bowl for sacrifice

I have learned the smell of the wild boar
and the whirl of the dance
I can enter the pool where the fish writhe
without their knowing
I have seen the four-horned deer
                proud on the hill's crest
in the dusk before dawn

I know how to dig out a broken thorn

to release the pain

and I have learned the words of the songs

*

father sent a messenger   a boy
light of weight   over the mire

too late   a host of warriors came
over the hill

on they ran like a wave of the sea
drowning everything
                    and with them the dogs of war

father was felled at the bend of the river
over the boom for the fishing grounds

his back was mauled   his body was in shreds

*

I am dressing myself to be given away
to a man I do not know

we will be tied together with a strip of hide
we will eat a stupid round flat cake
we will tell lies to each other and embrace

and so I am being born again   but I remember
everything that remains behind

*

now the clan is not even a rumour
now our tongue has shrivelled up

no one will hear our fame
our words are no more than wax in the ear

*

they say a great bird is coming
to soar over the rim of the earth
and cool the ground with its wings

even the dawn-caller will forget to awaken

*

it is not too far off
              the outermost time

when the world itself is thrown from a sling

when the Last of the Singers is gone

A Note on Grimspound

WE DO NOT KNOW what language was spoken in Grimspound at the time of its use or occupation. As an experiment in historical back-projection, all the poems in the fourth section of the text are derived from the *Nostratic Dictionary* (2008) compiled by the palaeolinguist Aharon Dolgopolsky. Nostratic is a hypothetical macro-family of languages that reconstructs the common origins of the known major language families of Eurasia: Indo-European, Semitic, Altaic, Kartvelian and Dravidian. In other words, it is a total fiction; but its basis in comparative philology gives it a plausibility hard to resist. And I have not resisted, which means that all the poems in the fourth section are based entirely on concepts and percepts found in the *Nostratic Dictionary*. The crucial factors in the cultural assemblage of Nostratic are judged to have been microlith technology, the use of the bow and arrow, and the domestication of the dog.

Inhabiting Art

Preface

INHABITING ART is a mode of being we all experience all of the time, without always remembering how the conditions we live in have been fashioned by cultural behaviour sometimes customary sometimes exceptional, sometimes unconscious sometimes intentional but always expressive of a *habitus*, a sense of being acquired in the company of others, in the everyday activities of a group whose shared ways of perceiving the world are the very ground of the individual vision, individual sensibility.

In this book, *habitus* is often tied to habitat, familiar territory seen in relation to familiar ways of making it work. Although I have a personal interest in natural history, these essays are about cultural history in relation to landscape and cityscape, cultural history viewed episodically or in the form of a palimpsest, where the present state of the habitat both reveals and conceals its own prehistory, the record of its own formation and transformations.

I am interested in artefacts that could only ever be the products of one place and one time, but equally I am fascinated by their ability to speak to us in our own languages of recognition and evaluation. They inhabit us when we extend to them the curiosity required to follow their rhythm, to home in on their pitch and tone of voice, and when our trust in them is sufficient to be able to inhabit the mysterious patterns they have imprinted on our imaginations. Some of these essays sound very knowing, but their own most continuous pattern is an insistence on what we don't know, whether the artefact in question is a simple utensil, a sophisticated oil painting, a neighbourhood, or a tract of forest.

The genre of the essay could be said to resemble a *habitus* in its own right, with an original habitat in the shape of Montaigne's tower, although this scene of writing was as much the construction of Montaigne's own imagination as of the skills handed down to his masons and carpenters; and this punctuating moment in cultural history is one pretext, or excuse, why these essays are also concerned with the play of the mind in every sense that the phrase can make room for.

Knife

It has a broad axe shape, but is sliver-thin. Even at the blunt end, the ochre-coloured flint, smoothed and polished, is a slim-line product. It looks like a small spatula, and would be something of a puzzle to archaeology, but speculation is pointless, rendered futile at a touch. The obliging object tells the hand exactly where it wants to go.

As soon as I picked it up, the long haft made itself at home, slung between first finger and thumb on the elastic webbing of skin. The first fingerpad went straight to the back of the blade. After three thousand years of dumb neglect, the instrument was attuned, responsive, prompt to its ancient cue.

The leading edge is minutely pecked. Broken small craters, overlapping scoops, were quickly opened up in the glassy stone by the same degree of force aimed repeatedly, dozens of times, at the same hard margin of a few fingers' breadth.

The life-knowledge of the flint-knapper dwells in the

sparing of exertion at the very point of landing a blow. The effects of this knowledge, the depth and shape of indentations in the stone, are accordingly generic if not uniform. An even more precise and unthinking calculation is needed for end-on strokes that split the individual flint.

At some point the maker, under the spell of making, no longer sees the use to which the blade is put, seeing instead the bloom of a new shape begin to emerge from the flint's uncertain depths. Sometimes this shape is only poorly divined, or glimpsed and avoided; sometimes it is nursed into life, by craftsmen who watch for the ideal form of knife-being, especially if this is a votive blade, intended for ritual deposit. Best of all is when the artist, setting his sights on perfect function, sees it rise above the horizon at the same point as beauty of form.

This tool for cutting was neither deposited nor lost. I think it was left beneath the roots of a broad oak with a clutter of flints, worked but unfinished, until the maker should return, and return soon. There it lay until the sea covered all the oaks whose stumps are now below the tides at Holme-next-the-Sea.

Lying there through storms that uncovered the massive inverted bole of roots at the centre of Seahenge, close by, it found another hand to belabour, to switch on, to gear up, when just enough sand had been swished aside for its pale surface to draw the eye.

It may never have been used, but was made for a hand that used others like it, and it would always transmit the same feeling for action, the same possible uses for butchery: severing, slicing, scraping. It was the lever between inner and outer worlds, it showed that the airs and waters, rocks and earth, moving and combining and resisting one another, obeying the spirits that ruled them, had their equivalent workings, their times of calm and upheaval, under the skin; in the wallowing lungs, the weeping flesh, the flowing heart, and in all the symmetries of bones and muscles, the asymmetries of lower organs, the random belt of the guts. It brought the cross-sections of life within grasp. Behind it, the physician's trial and error, the surgeon's initiative; the whole breathing, faltering body of science.

2003

Soluble Culture

Flag Fen, on the outskirts of an industrial estate near Peterborough, is a triumph of the invisible. One of the most important Bronze Age sites in Britain, it has neither the dramatic monoliths of Wiltshire or Orkney, nor even a bank, ditch, barrow or enclosure to mark the spot. Everything remains buried, apart from one small plot where the Bronze Age levels have been stripped of their cover and enclosed by a square brick hall. Inside, the material remains consist of several rows of three-thousand-year-old posts, alder and poplar, now dark and blasted but once the exposed tips of a timber platform stretching over water for one kilometre. Ten metres wide, the completed monument was an assemblage of over 66,000 posts, arranged into five rows. In use for some four hundred years, from about 1300 BC to 900 BC, its purpose was to make things disappear.

A religious recycling centre, the platform enabled the inhabitants of dry land to walk over water and consign their worldly goods to oblivion. Everyday objects in tip-top condition, flint tools and beautifully modelled pots, were dumped in huge quantities. High status ornaments and valuable weapons were deliberately smashed and decommissioned before being reassigned to another dimension, which is where the dead must live. The ancestors required food in the after-life, and so packed lunches were provided. Two completely unused quernstones were couriered over to enable them to grind their own corn. The point about all these votive offerings is that they were abandoned unconditionally, there was no cultural reclamation scheme, subsequent generations could not scavenge like metal detectorists, there were no Bronze Age repomen. It was only in fantasy, or in archaeology, that a hand would bring back Excalibur for a second chance, or that anyone would think of taking that chance.

The water began to rise after about 900 BC, and the whole edifice was drowned. Layers of silt accumulated steadily for over two and a half thousand years until the seventeenth century, when the long process of draining the fens was started. Channels were cut, guiding the water elsewhere, allowing the soils to dry, oxidise and blow away. At this point, the Wizard of Oz failed to turn up in East Anglia, and was filed away for another three hundred years. When enough soil had been exhausted, the felled timbers began to surface once more. The archaeology has left them in situ, but the situs is radically different. They are now cloaked in the spray of Anglia Water's 'innovative misting system', although this operates according to a rhythm of alternating showers and dry spells. The intermissions are extraordinary, when the silence begins to stage a comeback, as it thinks to do every few minutes, allowing the wood and mud to produce its own tiny capillary sounds. When this happens, you can hear the platform start to dream. It fully expects the whole process to shift into a different gear. The coordinates are scanned, the portals line up, the Stargate is about to open.

But there is no SG-1, no expeditionary force that did not go safely from one area of dry land to another. The passage between elements, between dimensions, was not a moving staircase designed by Powell and Pressburger. The journey was never undertaken, not even in imagination. The Bronze Age reconnaissance party was only ever given the practical task of sending objects down a conveyor-belt. They knew the experiment would go horribly wrong if you rearranged the molecular structure of personnel as well as utensils. Entering the portal, going over to the other side, is what we do now. But in case we should miss it, the Fenland Archaeological Trust has given us a sign: not 'Staff Only' but 'The Door to the Past'. The door requires a good shove: 'Enter and Step / Back in Time to the / BRONZE AGE.' First, we see the tangle of wooden piles enjoying their endless sauna; and then behind, or rather above them, on all four walls, a mural depicting the scene outside on a summer's day, three thousand years before the present. This painting is nearly as interesting as the prehistoric walkway, and after a while it is more interesting. Blatant, kitschy and as flat as a Julian Opie, it operates on the Tardis principle of giving an infinite extension to something shut in a box. Wherever you turn, you can see to the horizon. The painting is continuous through 365 degrees: over concrete blocks, under light switches and heaters, around exit signs. Its main effect is to make you stand still and absorb the details of a landscape that is not there — alerting the senses to sights, sounds and smells no longer available. The rituals of the Bronze Age would have suppressed this immediacy. The souls of objects were released into a muddy, obscuring medium, muffling all sound and extinguishing taste and smell. Sliding into the depths, they passed out of use and memory.

A more ambiguous door into the past swings on the hinges of the old Visitors' Centre. Although its replacement has been open for less than four months, this ancestral hall of wetland archaeologists is already suffering neglect. Only a quarter of its area is occupied by displays; the rest is a wilderness of outdated furniture and amplified plumbing sounds. It has the tranquillity of abandonment, broken suddenly by one burst of nervous laughter, coming from an unidentified source. The sound, which is cloaked and distant, is abruptly stifled. Like a conspirator in an English novel of the 1930s, this hidden day-dreamer is revelling in the details of a fantastic hoax, which members of the public must not know about. In any case, they only seem to stray in here by accident, nearly missing the extraordinary concentration of artefacts and residues of the Bronze Age farmer's encounter with cattle, pigs, sheep, goats, water-fowl, fish, eels, wheat, barley, hay, thatching, timber and peat. There is a wealth of domestic paraphernalia, but also an astounding display of fine metalwork, damaged but not ruined. Including a group of miniature swords of the late Wilburton type (900–800 BC) whose pale bronze sheen makes them look for all the world like a set of Mycenaean daggers. The polished armour of the beetle *Donacia impresa*, which feeds exclusively on bulrushes, tells an important story about the extent of wetland in the prehistoric epoch. It would have made the drovers curse, when their heavily laden carts got bogged down. The earliest wheel in Britain (1300 BC) is here, an assured piece of joinery whose tri-partite structure would have allowed for quick-fit mainte-nance. But Ministry of Transport inspectors aside (taking road tax where no tax has gone before), everyone else on site has turned into so much diverted traffic.

The focus is elsewhere, on the reconstructions. First up is the Iron Age roundhouse. I have been in this twice, and on both occasions there was the strong smell of a recent fire lingering around its tooled rafters. The light enters via pinholes in the roof and along horizontal shafts bursting through the door to pick out a series of superimposed modern bootmarks: 2001 Brashers, 2000 Meindls, 1999 Hi-Tecs – none of any real archaeological interest except perhaps the worn down prints of a pair of 1996 Timberlands. They bespeak some kind of ceremony carried out in the ash and dust and perhaps involving the vibrantly red mini-fire extinguisher. But the Iron Age is a polite afterthought at Flag Fen, where the real stock in trade is the alloys market. There is now a number of Bronze Age huts to choose from. Birds depart rapidly from the eaves as you enter the prototype. They have been caught taking Bronze Age roofing materials to heart, as well as to their nests. On my last visit, there was a nice new roundhouse next door, walls of hazel interlarded with a mixture of clay, straw and cow dung. The high finish to the plasterwork was needed for the curator's most audacious move, a series of speculative wall-paintings with geometric patterns. I realised suddenly I was in the showroom of a Bronze Age housing estate, and that a whole sector of the construction industry was poised for downsizing into Heritage. Outside grazed the simulacra of prehistoric sheep, trimming the edges of neat gravel paths, woolly exegetes of the universal aroma of manure. Laddish enthusiasts began to stake out the territory for a display of authentic skills such as hurdling and Australian-rules body painting.

Meanwhile, the archaeology continues to disappear. The cross-section of Roman road is as full of holes as a Swiss cheese produced under licence in Cheshire. A beehive has been established in the centre and nearer the bottom are several animal burrows. There is the powdered detritus of a sequence of miniature landslips. In the wood tanks, the water levels have dropped (there are condensation marks on the plastic sheeting). Exposed timber surfaces have started to fur over with moss. The pace of deterioration quickens into a legionaries' march. The only replenishments are those of plant species surviving from the Bronze Age: pondweed and great reedmace. Sedges flourish alongside flag irises, water plantains, water violets, purple loosestrife, devil's bit scabious and bog bean. The organic material crumbles, the strata bleed into each other. This is an inevitable process, part of the evolution of the site, which has taken on form and significance through a history of ramifying, syncopating, converging and diverging narratives and performances of loss and abandonment. Flag Fen is all about being resigned to a culture of giving things away. Disposable culture, relinquished, yielded up in a series of acts of surrender all held in solution, literally and figuratively.

But there is one set of artefacts that does not belong in the same scenario. Perhaps it did once, but it certainly does not now. This is the unique collection of timbers that composed the monumental circle of 'Seahenge', disclosed by a storm on the beach at Holme-next-the-Sea in October 1998. They are all there, the fifty-five posts that made up the circle around the massive central oak stump weighing two and a half tons. Sea water makes crystallised salt that damages prehistoric wood once it is unearthed, which is why English Heritage mounted a rescue operation to transport the various worked pieces of oak – and a honeysuckle rope – to wherever they could be studied properly. This had to be Flag Fen, and the research done has been meticulous and amazing, revealing that the great central stump was dislodged in either late spring or early summer of 2050 BC, when it was already two hundred and sixty years old. The total ensemble was hewn from between eight and fifteen trees, using broad-bladed bronze axes whose multi-directional strokes are individually fingerprinted according to irregularities in the metal.

But these massive fragments have been left in the morgue for nearly four years. And they have given up. The smaller posts, wrenched and bleeding, have sunk into deadness. The great altar, whose roots once pointed to the starlight, has been strapped down on its side. The trunk is striped with the flow channels of four years of douches, while the foam padding has become decrepit and addled with mould. It looks stunted, shrunken in on itself under loops of green piping and sacking off-cuts. There is enough green slime in the tank to bring you out in a cold sweat. I never thought I would say this, or think it, but the henge should never have been moved. It was part of a repertoire of sands and soils, of woods and waves, that gave it permission. It took its bearings from the masses and contours of the surrounding landscape, and in return it organised the materials and their meanings.

The latest fad among TV archaeologists in the era of the mixing desk is archaeo-acoustics. The idea is that certain neolithic and Bronze Age monuments, including the great chambered tombs and stone circles, have been given a structure that will resonate with particular frequencies, that will create the conditions for a certain pattern of sounds to be reproduced, even today. The spatial arrangements are what guarantee the time-links. I don't believe in this, but I can understand what motivates the thinking behind it. Monuments have only one context – which is not that of the earth they are mystically tied to: none of that pietism. The look and feel of the land have changed enormously over four thousand years, although it is still difficult to walk for an hour on the sands at Old Hunstanton, two miles further south, without counting the stumps of at least twenty neolithic trees. Location means belonging to a particular history of use, above all a history of giving, of letting go, in the terms of a social and religious economy

that seems alien to us even though it germinated the be-
ginnings of our own customs. Maybe it is only in the work
of the imagination that we can match the generosity of
that culture in its place. And if that is so: back to work with
a vengeance.

2003

Walking with Sebald

Sebald's work was diagnosis. When you got to the end of
The Rings of Saturn, you felt that you had been given a foren-
sic trail uncovering the steps leading to the ruined con-
dition of the European sensibility. And this was enough
to account for the state of near-paralysis suffered by the
narrator in the first few pages of the book. The first person
dominating this text – despite the many extensive passages
of ventriloquism – felt crippled personally by the chronic
wasting disease know as the European cultural tradition.
No other explanation was necessary. History was a burden
whose full weight was borne individually, and the more
one understood of it, the more one sank beneath its over-
whelming pressure. It was a brilliant stroke to issue this
report of a walking tour from a position of complete im-
mobility. It meant that the idea of travel, and the purpos-
es of travel, could be entertained first and foremost as a
journey of the mind. Sebald's itinerary along the Suffolk
coast was literally and metaphorically eccentric, missing
out several major foci of historical interest, including Al-
deburgh and Sutton Hoo. These and other omissions al-
low one to gauge something of his motivation in choosing
the particular tracts of country he explores in such detail,
even though the detail is rendered much more in terms

of historical associations than with regard to the physical reality of the landscape. Sebald pauses in his journey in order to recall the stories of individuals linked to specific places, and he is especially drawn to those episodes in their lives concerned with moments of choice, often of critical importance not just for one or two people, but decisive in the way they reveal the condition of an entire class, or the way of life of a sea-faring nation, or the collective psychology of an imperial power. This is a book of forking paths, a record of turning points in history, of the roads not taken. Sir Thomas Browne, Joseph Conrad, Chateaubriand, Edward Fitzgerald and Swinburne are among those figures who provide scenarios of diverging trails, and of misgivings that they have taken the wrong turning, that the route they have pursued has caused them to lose the lives they should have led. Sebald's own passage through the Suffolk countryside is constantly bedevilled by labyrinthine indirectness and actual mazes; he is thwarted by culs de sac and obliterated footpaths, turning this elegy for lost directions into a chronicle of anxiety.

The narrative commences with elegiac evocations of the characters and habits of three friends who have died within a short space of each other. The first two are scholars, the third a retired judge, but all three exemplify a complete immersion in the world of their study or contemplation, turning them into guardians of a body of knowledge, conduits for a particular current in intellectual or cultural history. When they die, an exceptional way of seeing the world dies with them, something that can never be replaced. Elsewhere in the book, it is not the tragic loss of individuals, but the slow death of entire families, the irreversible decline of complete industries, that appear to gather momentum in the telling. One of the most poignant reveries of all concerns the historical standing of the Ashbury family, residents of a large Irish country estate who cannot afford to defend their property against dilapidation. The physical deterioration keeps pace with the erosion of their will to survive and their ability to cope. Despite the inevitability of their eclipse, the narrator confesses his desire, formed during his short stay with them, to spend the rest of his life in the shadow of their bewildered stoicism, and this passage takes the full measure of Sebald's devotion to expired hopes and lost illusions. Even when the road not taken leads nowhere, it remains the occasion of lasting regret.

As the narration progresses, it thickens with the details of ways of inhabiting the landscape that have nearly all disappeared, and as it follows a course never very far from the Suffolk coast, it traces the outline of a constantly shifting threshold between land and sea. The East coast is where more of the English landscape has crumbled away than anywhere else. And the most spectacular marker of this vanishing territory is the town of Dunwich, once one of the busiest ports in the country, now reduced to the partial remains of a small complex of ecclesiastical buildings formerly on the very edge of town. But the lament for a lost landscape is even more profoundly felt in the remarkable section of the text concerned with the ecological trauma of 16 October 1987, when millions of mature trees, comprising the heart of Britain's ancient woodland, were devastated by hurricane force winds. Every adult in Britain now has a double focus on particular parts of the landscape, a before and after effect in their awareness of something missing that has to be supplied by the imagination. And this experience of loss is parallel to the émigré's feeling of dislocation from the landscape he grew up in, the environment in which the very template for his sense of landscape was formed. Perhaps this is why the human centre of the book seems to be provided by the narrator's visit to the home of another German-speaking emigrant, the writer Michael Hamburger, exiled from his native Berlin when only nine years old.

While the text is genuinely moved by the loss of physical features in the ensemble of town and country settings, of customs, ideas and personalities that it so scrupulously explores, it is arguing ultimately that landscape is something you carry around in your head, perhaps even more than it is something you encounter necessarily in your movement through a sensuous world. Perhaps this is why there is a high incidence of dreams in the text, since in dream it is common for the landscapes of one's past to be re-worked and combined. The writing fuses the log-book of a pedestrian journey with the flight of the imagination – its plotted itinerary keeps turning into an exploratory wandering. Just as the mind keeps pace with the body, and then moves away from it, so the text functions partly through retrieval and commemoration, partly through invention. Its strategy is reflected in the life-work of one of Sebald's heroes, the farmer Thomas Abrams, who has gradually abandoned farming – with the immediacy of its link to the landscape – in order to devote more of his time to the construction of a large-scale model of the Temple in Jerusalem. No one living knows what the Temple looked like, but the cultural imperative to remember its significance can only be achieved with an imaginative meticulousness otherwise known as love.

2002

Their Masters' Voice

The megaphones of Prague. There are still a few, here and there in squares such as Namesti Mim and I.P. Pavlova, reminding the passer-by with a jolt of the ways in which social space was controlled less than fifteen years ago. The anonymous voice of officialdom, projecting its designs into every corner of the city. The individual devices belie their function, coming in all shapes and sizes, anything but standard issue. In one respect, they are more out of place here than in any other city, since the cultural history of Prague is dominated by an iconography of alleys, hideaways, dark labyrinths, places to get lost in, rather than of open spaces and boulevards hospitable to crowds. The central figure in the nineteenth-century literature is that of the solitary wanderer, the *chodec*, who discovers the secret recesses of each quarter. Kafka drew the map differently, inserting this isolated figure within a geography of dread, showing how the reach of the authorities extends to every last passageway, culvert, waste lot. The successive bureaucracies of the Austro-Hungarian Empire and post-war communism took possession of the city of the alchemists and seized the right to speak for it, with a disembodied voice that is the ultimate expression of power whose interests are dislocated from those it claims to represent – the megaphone is the icon of the nomenklatura, political ventriloquists who do not speak with the people, but in their stead. At the same time, this mechanisation of the voice is intrinsic to a more clandestine tradition associated particularly with the area around the castle: with a belief in the golem, with a desire to create automata, with the dream of assembling a creature from disparate body parts. This rather more sinister genealogy was given official sanction by the paranoid collector, Rudolf II, who employed teams of magicians and who was delighted by any apparatus that simulated and displaced the human. Its artistic correlate can be found in the paintings of Arcimboldo, whose output is devoted to curious amalgams of objects that mimic the lineaments of the human figure. Nowadays, the electric wiring has been torn from every last speaker still in position, but it does not make any difference: the megaphones of Prague are forever earthed into a history, a memory reservoir, a cultural power supply. Easier to remove than the more obvious memorials to a future that never happened, they are mostly ignored, immobile, only rocking slightly with each change in the direction of blustering winds.

2003

End of the Line

Underground railways exist as alternative spheres to the cities they serve, they take on a character of their own, which we tend to think of in terms of rationalised space and time, as places where the unexpected is not meant to happen. The tube map with its symmetries, its rows of diagonals, its repetition of angles, is an excessive rationalisation of something that in reality is much more irregular. An accurate map would look worryingly chaotic, its proliferation of unrepeatable patterns would make the city look out of control. Where the tube ends is where the pattern most obviously unravels; it is where the dream of symmetry gives up. Most people never reach the end of the line where the idea of the city no longer obtains. Almost no one has travelled to the end of all the lines. That would mean being exposed to a degree of variety that the blueprint could never absorb. At every underground stop, people climb to the surface, emerge into the light of day, but the train goes on, the circulation continues, the Circle Line providing a visual and conceptual magnet for the way the city stays alive by pumping flows of energy around the system. At the end of the line this fiction dissolves; it is not only people but the place itself which releases its grip on the idea of the city as a closed system. Our project is an enquiry into what relates these different places apart from their entry into and exit from a system they are so iconically related to. Perhaps the termini are all portals into something other than the idea of the city we automatically link them with.

Of course, the Circle Line offers resistance, is in many ways in absolute contrast with the suburban tangents. There is no emergence, no aperture, except for those created during the Blitz, when bombs would come through the road above, or even bounce down the escalators, skip along the hallways and explode on the platforms. These violent incisions would not dispel the secrets of the entombed – the myth-making potential of all those repressed corridors – but would foster anew the sense of an alien habitat. This is caught most obviously by Quatermass and the Pit, where the breach into a deserted station uncovers the race-memory of another planet altogether. It is in the city's centre that the largest number of abandoned stations remains; there are forty altogether, repositories of gloom, amplifying the distant vibrations, allaying the slight breezes that pulse through the labyrinth, to decelerate as they get further and further away from the rushing air of tunnels where the trains still run. The lost stations comprise one extreme; the other consists of termini on the Central, Northern, District, Metropolitan and Jubilee lines: the ones that burrow furthest into another time, or into an entirely different organisation of space. And yet the tide-line of the city's history is indelible precisely here.

Morden has only been in pole-position as the southern end of the Northern Line since 1924, the year when Charles Holden crafted seven stations reaching out into the fields of Surrey. Now the terminus is under siege, filled up from within by a creeping lattice of iron scaffold poles, an infestation of plasterboard and yellow and black tape, which forces a savage geometry into the calm and carefully legislated spaces of Northern Line house style, the endless adaptations of white, green and black porcelain tiles. The platform indicators are bronze-edged lanterns, redolent of BBC Heritage, the reassurance of a Dock Green opening credit. But the lettering is both older and more modern than that post-Second World War community survivalism. The Johnston Sans typeface was first introduced in 1916, year of catastrophes, and yet seems to hold the clue to an ordered existence as economically and inevitably as a Bauhaus doctor's prescription. The real reason for journeying here is to visit the octagonal booking hall; and to leave here for any other destination is to unsettle a rare composure. People come and go looking down and straight ahead; but the space beckons upwards with a series of gestures, past the broad horizontal fluting of the gently pitched ceiling to a pinnacled skylight, whose glass panes are leaded in the form of a giant snowflake, a symmetry that has formed on its own. The entrance hall is made ceremonial by a startling, immensely simple, chandelier: a great brass circlet suspended by twenty-foot chains. The facade of Portland stone hints subtly at the ritual importance of setting forth, the commencement of a journey to the Underworld. Its two bas-relief columns share facets of Doric and Egyptian styles; but they are only allusions, not direct quotations like the stage-set pastiche down the road. The station came first, the rest of Morden curved away from it, but never quite matched up to the dignified arc of its approach road.

Direct competition came from above – Holden's design was totally crushed by three hideous stories added in the sixties – and from the corner of the road opposite, where the Portland stone was echoed, or rather amplified, in 1936, when a futuristic bulwark of a building was incised defiantly with a series of *fasces*; like the Party badge of a local financier dreamily hedging his bets.

Epping is not so much the end of the Central Line as the beginning of the Essex Way, that bucolic footpath winding a course as far as Harwich. The station wall sports a plaque celebrating the twenty-first birthday of this simulated Ancient Track. It has never been easy to decide where the Central Line should yield to the Forest. The Great Eastern Line (land-grabbed in the New Works Programme of 1935–40) had beached up in Ongar – three stops further out from Epping – in 1865; the first retrenchment came after the Second World War, when passengers for the Ongar outpost had to slip a loop in time, walking from one Epping platform to another to exchange their electric tube trains for steam. This concession vanished in 1970, when the last trails of coal-smoke disappeared with the surgical removal of Ongar, Blake Hall and North Weald – names redolent of the Squire's Last Stand and the primeval impasse. Epping represented a compromise between these feral sidings and an unidentifiable point nearer to Liverpool Street and the urban climax. Modernity was at the top of its bent with Gants Hill, whose concourse was modelled directly on the stations of the Moscow Metro – but Epping is already on the compost heap. It is a rural halt: convolvulus on wire netting, heavy laburnum, climbing roses, hanging baskets, blackberries. Local boys help old ladies with their suitcases. The old red-brick Victorian overland station is flanked by horse chestnuts, greenhouses and an allotment garden with runner beans and cabbages. It does not do to stand still for very long in Epping: spiders wander over my hands as I write on the parapet; a ladybird alights on my mobile phone. The line is closed off, but there is nothing to stop the trains from plunging forward in a rerun of Edward Upward's 1928 story, 'The Railway Accident' (Upward grew up in nearby Romford), except four red lamps planted – everything here is planted – on spindly metal poles in the middle of the tracks. One hundred yards further on, tall ragwort forms a screen as the rails begin to curve out of sight. The waiting room is different. It is the antechamber to a system that classifies everything in its vicinity. The suburbs as Mending Apparatus. The room possesses a single bench that faces a passport photo booth. Which is what the passengers wait for: their criminal typology; their Lombroso credentials. In Epping, the inhabitants conspire against the Greenwich Meridian.

At the western extremity lies Uxbridge, entombed in a future remembered by all those who were teenagers in the 1960s. The old market town, centred on a neoclassical colonnade, flagpole and clocktower, was falsified forever, rendered permanently asymmetrical, by the imposition of a concrete pavilion, the railway's version of South Bank brutalism. Inside the station, however, are the carefully antiqued remnants of a more homely brand of utilitarianism that was always more subtly disturbing. The wooden benches conjure up the era of Harry Palmer, the Michael Caine character for whom the most familiar objects turn suddenly very strange, and vice versa. In *The Ipcress File*, Palmer believes he is being held captive in Albania, but makes his escape onto the streets of London. Uxbridge is the Albanian version: all the artefacts are so convincing, so precisely evocative, they have to be stage copies. There is the original wooden refreshments kiosk, advertising the alternatives of A Mars A Day or CIGARS. The clock and platform indicator have a concatenating rhythm beyond the reach of the original design. It was an age of gadgetry, but the Uxbridge streamlining looks homemade. Pride of place goes to the four stainless steel cigarette machines, boasting their provision of DAY AND NIGHT SERVICE. The one going concern here is Frank's Coffee Shop, which still operates with the original sandwich board. Frank's message includes a prehistoric telephone number, consisting of two-letter prefix and five digits: UX 35489. Anyone phoning that number and expecting ring back will have one hell of a wait. Nowadays, the Underground itself is art; in the sixties, art and the railways had to be formally introduced – via civic heraldry and stained glass windows, job lots from Coventry Cathedral. But the most obdurate features of the design, the most aesthetically ambitious, are two extraordinary *couchant* abstractions of wheel and carriage, mid-way between rolling stock and Halley's Comet: these historical projectiles, coursing through the masonry like Hittite chariots, belong in a corridor of the Pergamon Museum, in the passage leading towards the monumental film sets of the Cold War period. The interior of the station is Portmeirion English: one of the lesser known studios of the British film industry. The props were all leased out from Shepperton in 1965.

Stanmore is way beyond the end of the line. The station is marooned, tipped into a gulley, by the constant backwash from a busy traffic artery. Its status is announced by a traffic island, covered by rampaging weeds that almost hide the entrance. There is an immensely long, incredibly steep staircase down to the platforms at the bottom of the hill. Pensioners can be seen puffing and pausing on every landing. This place was never anything but peripheral, a hill station that might be abandoned. The construction was only half-serious. Even the grandeur of the woodwork is wafer-thin. The station is surmounted by a loft conversion, with three dormer windows dressed with net curtains. But no one has ever moved into these corporate bedrooms, and further varieties of weed sprout from the chimney tops. At best, Stanmore is a depot for rolling stock, rather than a concourse for passengers. The vast shunting yards are empty, and the ten pairs of railway tracks are garnished with a thick rust. At the stroke of a pen, bureaucracy's finest decommissioned the plans before they were ever realised. All over the network are these tokens of *aporia*; behind the schedules and the signalling routines are strategic exceptions: the superfluous platform, the silent stairwell. Stanmore is the annexe of uncertainty, the shrine of second thoughts. It was never made redundant, but paralysed at a fixed point in the history of the Tube's development. Passengers climbing up and down the hill traverse the strata of transport archeology, with the platform level classified as the prehistory of railway heritage. No wonder the landings carry advertisements for the National Trust – history is no more difficult to access than boarding the train, and less of a nuisance. Nevertheless, that illusion of the British past we consent to is counterpointed by Police notices seeking help in the investigation of crimes of rape. The edifice begins to crack under the weight of these posters, blue plaques of unwillingness and immediate harm.

And so to Upminster, in the utter east. A spaghetti-junction of moving points, its visual clamour put to shame by the self-possession of a row of drainpipe boxes. Each is embossed with the date of their manufacture, 1931. This is the home of the so-called 'Underground Signal Box', an operations centre that oversees the migrations of millions of passengers, planning the flux and reflux of a daily cycle whose echoes reach as far as the station car park. There is a tideline of rubbish that ebbs and flows in the turning space before the main entrance. The Signal Box is a hot property, caged in, fenced off. Marc and I peer at its darkened windows, where shadows move close to the venetian blinds. These must be the shapes of the controllers, eying us up, shifting uneasily backwards and forwards, away from and towards the light. I avert my glance to the thick cast-iron of the bridge, which absorbs the last scraps of sunlight and is surprisingly warm to the touch. But Marc is pointing his camera at the tower and producing a small commotion. We do a quick march down the platform and out through the Victorian station building with its pointed brick arches and patched roof. The thing is, we already sound like anoraks, swapping choice items of information about the history of the railways; we know too much, and are going to pay for it. Visions of an airfield in southern Greece materialise suddenly. We exit smartly – past the end cottage with backdoor rowan tree – and size up the shopfronts. Upminster has a fetish for accuracy, for exact calibration: even the barber shop is called 'Martino's Precision Hairdressing for Men'. The first shop in the High Street proper is a joiner's and woodturner's, the 'Essex Centre' of woodcraft, from which the technology of modern transport sprang (from the work of wheelwrights, not from Essex). Britain had a radial system of carriers to London from the mid-seventeenth century, unique in Europe, and the prototype of the centrifugal/centripetal Underground network. A pristine culture of capitalism. The end of the line is always the next staging post; the culture of termini is always transitional, the organisation of space provisional. The western range of buildings on the High Street is conceived on a monumental scale, with pillars and capitals, and Egyptian details reminiscent of Morden in the south. An approach road to the metropolis, but only half of one, already half-cannibalised by thriving family businesses, just off-camera. Wealth has spilled out of the old moulds of class and profession, already a frozen memory when the architectural cousins of Howard Carter came metal-detecting in Upminster and put their finds in a living museum, evoking the earliest known urban planning tradition. We skirt a row of tethered Alsatians as each one stands up, sensing the approach of suspicious characters. There is no sanctuary in the church – the closed circuit television surveillance reaches as far as the high altar, and outside, in the churchyard elms, is a chorus of paranoid birdsong, several choruses, a veritable spaghetti-junction of alarm calls. Upminster is on guard; even the wildlife is recruited. The project is to stop the migration of meanings, arrest the flow of defining characteristics, to anticipate and prevent outsiders from rearranging the buffers, one cold rainy night.

Richmond wins the competition in property prices. In Richmond, you have arrived. The concourse houses the Richmond and Surrey Auction Rooms; you jump off the train and invest before you even get to the street. But something peculiar happens as you walk down the platform: there is a strange little overgrown patch of ground between the train and the station end of the railway tracks, where the line peters out. This small deposit of neglect, with its little pockets of chalk and different-sized gravels, has accumulated indifference at specific moments of alteration and redefinition. It is a transport midden, a municipal burnt mound – by-product of energies that were focussed elsewhere. Like time-lines in the Thames foreshore, the overlapping of materials is constantly revised, realigned by the superimposing of new layers; the addition of elements reorganises the entire existing order of monuments. But the evidence of power-play is not enshrined in the canonical details of a metal-framed clerestory, or an abstracted

Egyptian facade; it is preserved in a pile of detritus. Its obsolescent mass, undesigned and unamenable to design, is conspicuously ignored. It is meant to be invisible, but its formlessness is reflected, magnified and distorted by the huge mirrors at the other end of the platform, convex and enveloping like an end-of-the-pier amusement. Richmond has seven platforms. The central two, with cast iron pillars, capitals and trefoils, are original, while the rest, with forged steel equivalents, repeat the blue and grey colour scheme, but shift the tones and textures. The most dramatic recension is not only recent, it is still in process. South West Trains are installing a 'Real Time' Customer Information System. But the Tube journey is never in real time; it is subject to dilation, a time exposure, as Marc's photographic activities constantly remind me. As the motion of the body through space accelerates, the mind dwells on its captivity, lapsing into the same condition between different stations. The first Underground railway carriages were called 'padded cells': there were no windows, because it was judged there was nothing to see. Not even the staging posts. The mind was confined within itself.

On the front of Richmond station, the sharply angled fluting above Egyptian-style pilasters completes the web of allusions, north, south, east and west, to Middle Kingdom architecture. But this grandiosity, although heavily suggestive, is less structural, less integral, to the Tube than the hieroglyph, the graffito awaiting its Rosetta Stone. The carriages are full of cartouches which preserve a code of silence about the true names for all the destinations. Morden is really 'Ammo City', but there is no knowing why. The Underground is a place where we read, unceasingly, a series of mottoes impacted with meanings which do not belong there. Surreptitious, sidling, they appear with the force of revelation, but reveal only the banal, like the scribbled *communiqués* of the Duke of Portland in Mick Jackson's novel *The Underground Man* (Picador, 1997). The Duke, who has constructed a system of tunnels beneath his estate, allowing him to travel by coach and horses for miles underground, slips an assortment of notes under the doors of his manservants and maidservants – conundra, such as 'What is that state of mind we call "consciousness" if not the constant emerging from a tunnel?' In the tunnels of the Victoria Line, nearly all the current advertisements are rudimentary and without entertainment value. Their most important message is the website address you can click onto to see the real advertisement. The only perspective here is a cyberspace perspective. When we emerge from the tunnel at the end of the line, we walk from terminus to terminal, enter a tunnel much longer than any we have just left. The underground from which we emerge into consciousness is unbearably private: without the freedom of the street, it fosters an intimacy with strangers that was the paradoxical ground of wartime myths of community. Travelling blind in this short space has an imagined scope unimagined in the endless suburbs of the Net. Digitised fantasy always needs to be fleshed out by actors; holograms stalk the green belt, the garden cities and country parks. Each padded cell is its own world, its own itinerary of symptoms: read your ticket for the precise aetiology, the carved channel you have travelled in secret, the time-signature of the gradients. Hold your breath until the journey ends, and your name is off the critical list.

2003

A Wild Nursery for the Arts
the site of the V&A

The V&A collections started life in places quite other than South Ken: in the Government School of Design at Somerset House in 1837, and then in the Museum of Manufactures and the Museum of Ornamental Art established at Marlborough House in 1852. It was not until the Commissioners for the Great Exhibition of 1851 began to acquire land in order to realise Prince Albert's grand design of collecting together in one place the national museums, the headquarters of learned societies and a scientific and technical university, that the present site of the V&A was secured. The collections were boosted by exhibits from the Great Exhibition and were reopened as the South Kensington Museum in 1857, although the permutating architectural solutions to the problem of display were not stabilised until 1899.

Before the Crystal Palace, with its six million visitors, was erected on Rotten Row at the south of Hyde Park, the area comprising Brompton and Kensington had been quiet for a thousand years. At the time of the Domesday survey, it was a paradise of pigs. The inhabitants of Chenesit (Kensington) in 1086 included eighteen villeins, one priest, seven bondsmen and around two hundred hogs. The large acreage given over to pannage connoted extensive woodland, although there was also agricultural land with work for ten ploughs, and a vineyard. Property values were high even then, with Kensington almost at the top of the Saxon and Norman real estate league table. The asking price for the whole area would have been ten pounds (compare Islington at ten shillings).

According to Walter Besant, in the relevant volume of his *Survey of London* published in 1911, the name Brompton is derived from 'Broom-town', 'carrying suggestions of a wide and heathy common'. If this is rather fanciful (at least some of the land was cultivated, since there was a Broom Farm in the vicinity in 1294) it nonetheless reflects faithfully the way in which the area was perceived up to the eighteenth century. At the time of Domesday, the land was owned by the Church (actually, the Bishop of Constance) and it remained in ecclesiastical hands throughout the Middle Ages. This almost guaranteed resistance to development, as with many London suburbs before the Reformation, and is part of the reason why the pre-nineteenth century story of Brompton (the name South Kensington was not in use until the 1850s) is less about the frontier between the urban and the rural than about the rivalry between nature unkempt and nature controlled.

After 1675, Brompton became quite literally the most cultivated place in England, with the establishment of the first nursery garden in the country. This enterprise was to dominate horticultural practices nationally, and soon achieved an international reputation. But before that, Brompton was wild. Very wild. Pepys even thought it dangerous, recounting a journey taken on 15 June 1664, from Somerset House to Kensington, in terms that are almost scare-mongering: 'But, Lord! the fear that my lady Paulina was in every step of the way: and indeed, at this time of the night, it was no safe thing to go that road; so that I was even afraid myself, though I appeared otherwise.' Even seventy years later, in 1734, Lord Hervey was writing to his mother in similarly melodramatic vein, giving her to understand that Kensington must be entirely cut off from the capital: 'we live here in the same solitude as we should do if cast on a rock in the middle of the ocean, and all the Londoners tell us there is between them and us a great impassable gulf of mud.'

Yet by the time that Hervey was writing, this intimidating wilderness was cheek-by-jowl with the most systematically managed landscape anywhere. The most celebrated of the new commercial plantations was the Brompton Park Nursery, precisely on the present site of the V&A. Founded by George London, in 1681, this was reckoned to supply most of the nobility and gentry in the country with trees, shrubs and plants. By 1715, Stephen Switzer was calling it 'the noblest Nursery of the world'. John Evelyn was a huge fan, recording in his diary for 24 April 1694 a visit undertaken to impress his acquaintance, Mr Waller, who was 'in admiration at the store of rare plants and the method he found in that noble nursery and how well it was cultivated'. The recurrence of the epithet 'noble' is motivated partly by appreciation of the orderliness and grandeur that distinguished Brompton Park from its competitors, but also by association with the status of its customers. At the height of its operations, the nursery covered over a hundred acres, while the scale and variety of the stock was nothing short of 'incredible', according to John Bowack, writing in 1705 in his *Antiquities of Middlesex*: 'if we believe some who affirm that the several plants in it were valued at 1d apiece, they would amount to above £40,000.'

It was because of this horticultural background, and the degree of its success, that Brompton was chosen as the prospective site for an architectural project that, had it been realised, would have fixed forever the character of the whole area and rendered impossible the future development of the V&A. The plans, drawn up in 1836, envisaged the construction of the largest market in the world, in the form of a huge triangle of neoclassical colonnades, wedged into the angle formed by the Brompton Road and Knightsbridge. The promoters of the Knightsbridge Market Company entered into a collaboration with the Birmingham,

Bristol and Thames Junction Railway to bring the nearest railway line to a terminus at Knightsbridge Green. The idea was not simply to provide a distribution point for the produce of Brompton, but to create a nexus 'to which the produce of the north and west of England, of Wales, and Ireland, as well as that of the market gardens about Hammersmith and its vicinity, can be brought with the greatest rapidity and at the smallest possible cost'. The prospective shareholders anticipated, eagerly, a 'great pre-eminence over every other metropolitan market yet established'.

No museums, no concert halls, no universitie −; no South Ken. The whole of Brompton would have resembled a giant garden centre annexed to a mammoth supermarket. There is no trace of the developers' plans today, but there is plenty of evidence of the burgeoning plant life that the place was once famous for. It is now corralled, isolated, dispersed, but there is still a great deal of herbaceous extravagance and variety in the streets, mews and gardens behind the V&A: in the figs and bay trees that line the approach to Holy Trinity Church; in the fuchsias, magnolias and agapanthi of the gardens behind Brompton Square; and in the dozens of terracotta tubs that line Ennismore Garden Mews. The tiniest cubic area of soil is enough to support the most ambitious of vegetable careers. Perhaps the most impressive example of plant mind over matter is the sizeable laburnum sprouting out of the top of the Corinthian capitals at the entrance to Ennismore Garden Mews.

More or less immediately west of the present Exhibition Road is where the gardens finished and the groves began. The great reformer Wilberforce, living from 1808 to 1821 at Gore House, on the site now occupied by the Albert Hall, was a world away from the busy transactions to the east: 'We are just one mile from the turnpike at Hyde Park Corner, having about three acres of pleasure-ground around our house, or rather behind it, and several old trees, walnut and mulberry, of thick foliage. I can sit and read under their shade with as much admiration of the beauties of nature as if I were two hundred miles from the great city.' An awareness of this atmosphere of bucolic remoteness makes it seem slightly less incongruous that Wordsworth should have married Mary Hutchinson in Brompton, on 4 October 1802. The sense of arboreal seclusion is what was cherished, and its loss lamented, when the museum-builders set to work. The newspapers of the day decried the loss of the Kensington 'wilds', and the destruction of their 'green lanes.' green lanes' where various kinds of game birds could be found, especially snipe and partridge. As an alternative tactic, it was also argued that the terrain was quite unsuitable for museums, since the neighbouring 'swamps' with their prevailing mists would affect adversely any works of art on display. But this claim seems likely to have been exaggerated since Brompton had for some time enjoyed the reputation of being one of the most salubrious places in Britain. It was warm, but well-ventilated, and for this reason was chosen in 1841 as the site of the new Hospital for Consumption and Diseases of the Chest. We would balk nowadays on hearing the description of Brompton as the 'Madeira of London', but by 1871 it had achieved a mortality rate even lower than that of Cheltenham, at that time reckoned to be the healthiest place in the country.

The green lanes and the groves for contemplation seem very distant today from the Cromwell Road and Cromwell Gardens, with their scabby London planes ringed around with cigarette butts. However, there are a few hints remaining of the kind of tranquillity that Wilberforce enjoyed: in the padlocked stillness of Ennismore Gardens; in the umbrageous canopies of Rutland Gate; most of all, in the graveyard of Holy Trinity, now almost entirely stripped of graves, and pacified by an avenue of horse chestnuts and stripling beeches.

Just as the collections of the V&A reveal the evolution of the museum's character, the story of its surroundings is equally palimpsestic. There are pockets of traditional usage, whether of window-box nursery cultivation, or of urban set-aside; but perhaps the most vibrant tradition is that of the Great Exhibition itself. The V&A is now home to many of the 1851 exhibits, but the internationalism of the original event is best represented outside the museum walls: in the multicultural student body of Imperial College; and in the diversity of the nearby churches. Besides the Anglican Holy Trinity, there is the towering Brompton Oratory (the land was bought in 1852, despite the objections of Cardinal Newman, who shrank from the idea of building in this 'neighbourhood of second-rate gentry and second-rate shops') as well as the Mormon temple with its pyramidal lightning rod, earthing the faith of the Latter Day Saints, and the wonderful golden facade of the Russian Orthodox Church of the Dormition of the Mother of God and All Saints, with its oddly Italianate bell-tower. Foreign consulates are thick on the ground in this area, with limo-cleaning chauffeurs beating their rubber floor mats against the porch of the Russian church, which is a near neighbour to both the Embassy of the Sultanate of Oman and the People's Bureau of the Great Socialist People's Libyan Arab Jamahiriya. The cosmopolitanism of 1851 survives, although its character has changed. In the nineteenth century it was provided mainly by waves of actors, musicians and writers colonising the streets of Brompton. One of the most notable visitors was the great French poet Stéphane Mallarmé, who stayed at 6, Brompton Square in 1863. By that time the South Kensington Museum would have been fully in operation, although it would have looked quite different from what we see today, housed as it then was in the notorious 'Brompton boilers', constructions of corrugated metal, glass and iron girders that were eventually removed to Bethnal Green, where they still form an integral part of the Bethnal Green Museum. South Kensington was to change its shape several times before the twentieth century: no longer green or tilled or quiet, except in those odd corners that George London would have appreciated, or the author of L'aprés-midi d'un faune.

2004

Atkins/Warsaw

Marc Atkins is best known for his photographs of London. Several of these were published in the collaborations with Iain Sinclair, Lights Out for the Territory and Liquid City, but they represent only a handful of the reputed 30,000 images of the city that he has created. These urban icons should be seen alongside the other aspects of his oeuvre: portraits (eleven of these, chiefly of maverick writers, are housed in the National Portrait Gallery); and dreamed-of scenarios and narratives – the most mysterious and least well-known area of his work. With his latest publication, Warsaw, arousing huge curiosity in the Polish capital, he has returned to urban iconography in a way that clearly invites comparison and contrast with his representations of London. The choice of subjects in the later series reflects a desire to reframe the earlier work as part of a structure of correspondences. It becomes possible to pair off single images and groups of images as mutually defining.

One of the most revealing comparisons brings together the funerary traditions epitomised in studies of individual tombstones. The London variants are among Atkins's most celebrated images; they show crumbling stone, infested with decay, absorbed into and overcome by organic growth which mimics and subverts the forms of statuary and stonemasonry. The monument's passage through time is characterised by friction and granulation. In Warsaw, the stone is polished; marble is used, or composite emulations of marble's smoothness, memorialising not so much the manner of death – as is common especially in eighteenth century inscriptions in Britain, recording the progress of the body's disintegration and the soul's resolution – but a phase of existence long before the moment of decease, during a period of health, vitality and self-possession. This aura of immunity is captured in a small portrait photograph that is sealed with a hard glaze, in a culture where the enshrining of the relic was superseded by the preservation of Lenin's tissue. The architecture of death is cryogenic in Eastern Europe. It is the architecture of the everyday that is subject to dramatic forms of abrasion.

Image after image in the Warsaw series shows the flux and reflux of history: history hurrying in opposite directions; backwards and forwards at one and the same time. Large areas of the city are feral. Ill-kempt and overgrown farmland survives less than a mile from the city centre; Atkins focuses on an agricultural penthouse, typical of the improvised architecture of the countryside, its only gesture to modernity an array of different-sized plastic buckets, the most modern of materials being utilised for the most primitive of necessities. The land-use demonstrated in the shadow of soviet-style tower blocks and the cranes of present-day construction adheres to the traditional mixed economy of the village. While one half of Polish society prepares for global postmodernity, the other half retreats into a subsistence recess. This photograph is not so much elegiac as prophetic: of a modernity that is less and less totalised, more and more likely to be cannibalised for spare parts; of history as a setting for divergences, which seems to be the implication of Atkins's study of the Old Town, that epitome of post-war reconstruction, the occasion of national pride and self-confidence, portrayed here as a focus of uncertainties, a multi-perspectival grid of shifting points of view, absent vistas – a secret desire for *impasse*.

The Atkins obsession with infrastructure, with competing forms of transit and transport, is distilled in a portfolio of depictions of empty or under-used thoroughfares. This badly lit and vacated modernity, often jerry-built or apparently unfinished bears a family resemblance to Ilya Kabakov's 'We Live Here Now', an installation in which the grandiose ambitions for a technologised future are abandoned by workers who live out their days in the prefabricated huts intended for use only during the period of construction. Atkins's representations of Warsaw push hard at the paradox of grossly overcrowded private space absorbing a stereotypical Polish gregariousness, while a false communality is identified with the unwanted abundance of public fora and meaningless concourses. A junction of darkened boulevards, catering to buses, trams and even cycle paths, is completely deserted except for two waiting pedestrians, whose twilit vigil is at the centre of a seemingly entropic system, with the batteries of modern city life running low, and the schematic outlines of bicycles curiously miniaturised marking the foreground like police records of a presence gone forever.

This Warsaw is a city of disappearances, of a history leaching out through the stone and brick of a fabric that could not be more distressed, whose patched and stained facades offer maximum resistance to the wipe-clean surfaces of modernity. In a city whose foundations lie in sands and gravels, the archaeology is all above ground, the record of past conflicts only skin-deep beneath a thin layer of badly mixed plaster, apparently designed to fall away in time for each generation to have to rehearse its own strategies for oblivion.

In many ways, the most haunting of these images is Atkins's Breughel-equivalent version of a new Babel, a monument to unrestrained ambition, to the desire for endlessly upward mobility that could not be more weighed down. This is his portrayal of the new television centre. The amount of pressure per square centimetre bearing down on this structure is like that on the ocean floor. But this solidified vacancy, this shrine to the dead zone, is also something else; it is the Colosseum, exactly as dreamed of by Hitler. It was only after the visit of Hitler and Albert Speer in the 1930s that the Colosseum was cleared of the centuries-old colonies of flora and fauna that had learned to live in its shadow, including several unique species. All this had to disappear when the building became the blueprint for a new culture, for a barbarous form of civilisation in which a ruin becomes the image of the future, not the image of the past; not a place that shows all the evidence of many cycles of growth and decline, of a process of continuous change. Photography is often thought of as a medium that fixes the moment, cryogenising it for future generations, but it can also become the means of showing how nothing is ever fixed, how the moment will always elude us, how all that can be recorded is irrevocable loss. And it is somewhere in the shifting sands between those two positions that Marc Atkins's work is situated.

2003

Lares et Penates

The road to Barjac, the hilltop citadel where Anselm Kiefer has his living and working space, is long and serpentine if you approach it from Nimes. Nimes is the ideal starting-point for this journey, its antiquity making it an icono-graphical primer for many of Kiefer's preoccupations. Among its Roman remains, the amphitheatre in particular (standing in for the Colosseum of the early photographic sequence, Heroic Allegories) pays homage to a painter whose architectural spaces often remind us of the fatal legacy of the imperial idea, with its double dream of order and bar-barism. But it is not this that makes me queasy so much as the lurching drive through the vineyards, in a business-class Mercedes piloted by an air-brushed lady chauffeur. I want to throw up, but am conscious that in this milieu, us-ing a Mercedes as a vomitorium would brand me as distinctly vulgar, if not an absolute barbarian.

But it's OK. We are there and I am already inflating my lungs with the healthful South, with scents of pine, laven-der, rosemary. The air of Provence in April, nothing more tonic. Of course, this airiness is not what Kiefer's work is about, and it is not, ultimately, what Barjac is about. If in one sense the hilltop complex is a vast depot, a concate-nated series of magazines in which paintings and objects accumulate, a concentration of German DNA distilling pa-tiently in a southern landscape, it is also a vast marshalling yard, from which a series of epitomes of an entire world are despatched to another dimension, that of the remote portals of the art gallery circuit with its forms of restless public attention, drawn fitfully to Kiefer's works via equal amounts of curiosity, suspicion, fear and deep recognition. Those who view Kiefer's work do not easily forget it. Its imprint is decisive although its meanings remain hard to focus. Barjac feels very distant from the art world's practices of exposure and mediation – the principles on which it has been conceived and constructed are those of retraction, withdrawal, self-reflection. It is not meant for public consumption, although its arrangements disclose a system of relations and a means of classification that make sense of decades of artistic activity.

Kiefer's front drive is a kind of ceremonial way. Once through the security gate, you follow a route that girdles the summit of the hill, a small plateau in which the main holding areas are located. The mild gradients of this approach road, really a wide path, encourage a slow, almost stately, walking pace, suitable for meditation or for the tempo of a procession. The latter option springs to mind once you begin to register that there are stations on this route, a series of structures that resemble cultic buildings, with their walls much taller than they are wide, housing small installations of paintings and sculptural objects. Each of these artistic precincts is named for a figure or theme that occupies an important role in Kiefer's imagination: 'El Cid', 'Vergil', 'Vanitas', 'Asteroids', 'The Seven Palaces', etc. Many of them refer to celestial systems, described in either scientific or mythological terms, while others commemorate moments in political or cultural history that serve as indices of humankind's attempt to draw heaven down to earth, or emulate it, with disastrous results. The most recently completed structure, 'Velimir Khlebnikov', shares the same inspiration as Kiefer's new show at White Cube, exploring the Russian poet's theories of history, using mathematics to uncover its laws and to predict the course of future events.

There is a necklace of these shrine-like buildings looped around the curving approach to the centre of operations. They bring to mind Dante's description of the hilltop town of Monteriggione, its circle of walls 'crowned with towers' (*Inferno*, xxxi, 41) resembling the upper halves of giants peering over one of the pits of Hell. This analogy to the infernal scene is not a casual one. Just as the Italian hilltop town is displaced by giants in Dante's imagination, so these architectural superstructures are paralleled in Kiefer's scheme by the cavities beneath them, deep down, in the tunnels and grottoes that run in all directions through the wooded ridge. Should you enter this network of underground spaces, irregularly lit from artificial, and occasionally natural, sources, you would soon lose your bearings and, perhaps especially, your sense of the depth to which you have penetrated beneath the surface of the landscape. At what you feel instinctively is the lowest and the focal point of this ensemble of burrows is the experience of a sudden gap, an intensified vacancy, given the form of a great square chamber, lined with lead, half-filled with water and illumined bleakly by a single bulb. Viewed in any context, this is a scary place. Perhaps its most disturbing aspect is not the fleeting thought that this sacral pool is a symbolic space echoing a profound deadliness inside Kiefer's own head (he is actually a very friendly man with a sunny smile) but the more certain belief that it embodies the conditions of a widely shared psychological state, of a cultural memory and a national trauma. It is not for nothing that Kiefer's staff refer to it colloquially as the 'bunker', encapsulating the historic fate of the most expansive and all-embracing of political ambitions, reduced to a state of entombment and asphyxia, the exhaustion of light and air.

The stillness, darkness and coldness of this place could not be further from the thyme-filled atmosphere of the French countryside, or, for that matter, from the play of breezes in a spacious avenue of linden trees. The unusual sense of pressure experienced at this relatively shallow depth below ground is owing largely to the use of lead. Lead is one of the most frequently used materials in Kiefer's practice as an artist, at least for the last quarter century, during which time its implications have varied although certain emphases have remained constant. Lead is the base metal from which the alchemist aspires to produce gold. Kiefer's interest in alchemy has centred in the metaphorical resonance it has for his own painting, although he has also taken seriously the spiritual ambitions of the alchemist and his vision of parallel universes. The artist told me he had been 'persecuted for years' by a dictum of Robert Fludde: 'everything on earth has its equivalent star in heaven'. This conception of nature as reflecting a cosmic order gives value and coherence to the base, material existence of humanity even if cannot be grasped by the individual consciousness. On the other hand, the spectral correspondence produces restlessness and dissatisfaction, incessant striving of the intellect to outreach its limitations and possess its heavenly equivalent. That way, madness, the Faustian wager and the will to power. Kiefer uses lead most spectacularly in his atlases of the stars, cross-sections of the galaxy visible from earth. The relations between individual stars are proposed in the tracing of geometrical diagrams, while at the foot of the painting, the surface material is torn aside to reveal an underlying representation of architectural structures on earth repeating the same proportions. These structures are often modelled on the observatory buildings at Jaipur, themselves monumental equivalents of hand-held astronomical instruments. The scaling up and scaling down holds in tension idealism and self-delusion. The plane of the stars is represented on sheets of lead, suggesting that the material the artist hopes to spiritualise is finally recalcitrant and non-convertible, and that his attempts at transformation are liable to back-fire. The stars themselves are denoted by their astronomical numbers, reflections of a NASA project whose insane drive for completeness in an infinitely expanding universe is ironised by the deposits of number tags collecting in drifts beneath paintings and elsewhere on site. The final degradation is the silting up of these fallen stars in run-off channels and drainage gutters.

Kiefer's design for Barjac translates into three-dimensional form the obsessions of so many of his paintings that divide their attention between the material and the spiritual, the terrestrial and the celestial, the historical and the mythical. Dominating the entire property is the most grandiose and ambivalent fabrication of all, the prototype of the stage design for the 2003 production of Richard Strauss's opera, *Electra*, at the Teatro San Carlo, Naples. This gigantic structure consists of four tiers of fluted concrete, arranged as a series of terraces, like the enormous mould of an inverted ziggurat. As a building project, it reaches higher than anything else at Barjac, yet is organised around an immense and inexorable downward pull that expresses the fortunes of the house of Atreus and, more generally, a sense of history as dilapidation, as a series of narratives the more vulnerable the greater the scale of their ambition. One gets the feeling that if he could have done, Kiefer would have constructed it of lead. The whole building is a plummet, dragging the viewer down into its depths, just as the cistern beneath it reflects in its leaden ceiling the imagined plane of the stars. Nothing at Barjac rests on its own level. Kiefer is still adding to the design, drawing new buildings onto the existing plans, tunnelling into previously untouched areas of the hillside. Each move tightens the system of cross-references. Occasionally, we see the satellites of this system crossing our paths through the art world, but this is the constellation to which they naturally return.

Spatial Utopias

Earlier this year, the Kabakov habitat was altered dramatically when the immense beech tree overshadowing their house on Long Island began to disintegrate. The dryads had fled. The once protective canopy became an arboreal juggernaut that had to be stopped in its tracks. Regretfully, the artists commissioned a team of axe-murderers, who made the last act of *The Cherry Orchard* look like a posse of boy scouts gathering tinder. It is possible that this tree provided inspiration for a vocabulary of 'trunks' and 'branches' peppering the Kabakovian descriptions of the utopian city that forms the main reference point for the exhibition opening at the Albion Gallery in October. The utopian city is, or should be, constructed over one of the 'energy centres' of the earth. These are places in which the energy of the globe itself is concentrated and augmented by an invisible vortex, an imaginary lens capturing the energy that radiates from the cosmos. The architectural and metaphysical scope of the Albion Gallery projects is staggering, and seems wildly disproportionate in the context of the Great Peconic Bay. The Kabakovs' domestic and studio spaces are restrained – theirs is a generic Long Island property made with wooden shingles, overlooking a shallow arm of the sea criss-crossed by dinghies and canoes. But behind the stereotypical facade, an unceasing flow of new concepts is generated. In a sense, all the spatial containers of the Kabakovian imagination are generic; even those installation scenarios that employ autobiographical material are based on a selection of typical rather individualising memories. The recurrent paradox in the oeuvre is that stereotypical houses are inhabited by comrade citizens all of whom are idiosyncratic participants in 'fantasy production'. Their secret lives do not reflect what is psychologically unique, but project the desire for a universal condition of being, an idealised, utopianised version of the standardisation of Soviet life that the Kabakovs' art both focuses on and aims to transcend.

In conversation, Ilya Kabakov is at pains to underline the extent to which his art does not reveal his own personality but represents an assimilation to the point of view of the reader or viewer. Placing the emphasis not on the point of origin of the concept but on the moment of reception has been characteristic of his installations from the beginning. The 'Ten Characters' that feature in his earliest major installation are fictitious residents – seemingly chosen at random – of a typical communal apartment. They are all average citizens, but they are simultaneously artists dreaming of invisible worlds. They include Kabakov's first installation-protagonist, 'The Man Who Flew into Space from his Apartment', a figure who first appeared, or who failed to appear, in the artist's own Moscow apartment, where the evidence for his departure was represented by a giant catapult suspended beneath a hole in the ceiling. Much of the subsequent output, whether of Ilya working solo, or of Ilya and Emilia operating in tandem, has comprised an expansion in scale of this early scenario, since a whole range of later projects has been attributed to fictitious characters, to imaginary personae, and even to pseudonymous substitutes for the originators themselves.

Perhaps the most dramatic and ambitious demonstration of the latter form of contrivance took place in the recent Cleveland exhibition that proposed an 'alternative history' of Russian painting in the twentieth century. The alternatives were all dreamed up by Ilya himself and took the form of three separate artists that he had invented: Charles Rosenthal, Ilya Kabakov and Igor Spivak. Rosenthal came equipped with a biography that made him a student first of Chagall, then of Malevich, that associated him with a positive use of figurative realism during the utopian phase of the soviet experiment, and that killed him off in 1933. 'Kabakov', confusingly, was not the same as the installation-artist called Kabakov, but a follower of Rosenthal, inspired by photos of his mentor's paintings, and active mainly in the 1970s. Perhaps the most dizzying aspect of this duplication of identities was the dating of pictures painted, for example, by 'Kabakov' in 1972, but also by Kabakov in 2002. Last in the series was Spivak, born in 1970, an unwilling postmodernist whose work was filled with nostalgia for the conditions in which the first generation of soviet artists had worked, and whose segmented style based on the fragmentation of media photographs derived from the observation of torn-off strips of newspaper used as toilet paper in communal apartments. The extraordinary scope and variety of this exhibition, whose scale did indeed suggest the resources of three separate lifetimes' worth of production, unsettled the relationship between style and authorship, and between representation and expression, in quite profound ways, creating deep unease among collectors unwilling to purchase canvases by Rosenthal and Spivak that did not also bear the signature of Kabakov. Even greater uncertainty might have been generated had the Kabakovs been able to carry out their recently devised plan of selling off Ilya's estate in advance of his own death. The disposal of property and use of the proceeds to establish a foundation would have severed the link, conceptually at least, between the work and its biographical stimulus.

The 'parabola' of Russian art in the twentieth century, as interpreted in Kabakov's 'alternative' history, reaches away from realism and reflection in the direction of idealism and projection. Kabakov stresses the superiority of unrealised projects to all those conceptions that were actually given concrete form. In political terms, fantasy production is preferable to the spatial embodiment and temporal performance of ideas. For the artist working in three dimensions, the best solution is the maquette. For the curator, the goal should be to reinvent the museum or gallery as a storehouse for fantasies. The mutual abrasion of haunting fantasy and brutal realism has been encapsulated most economically in *The Red Wagon*, now installed permanently at Wiesbaden, where a cramped and rudimentary housing, seemingly neglected, encloses panoramic visions and obsolete chorales inspired by a sense of collective purpose. A conspicuous amount of the Long Island studio space is devoted to archives, a library, storage. Moving slowly from one area to another, one is conscious of the accumulation of desires, not just of individual sensibilities, but of an entire culture, the symbolic deposits of a way of life that dominated half the planet not so long ago, but which already seems strangely remote. One particularly large room is filled with maquettes, many for projects which are never to be realised. They tap into a reservoir of dreams that were the myths of at least three generations. A similar focus on the power of dreaming is at the core of the Kabakovs' design for their new installation soon to be unveiled at the Serpentine Gallery. A radial plan is dominated by an array of couches on pedestals that prepare the viewer to imagine a ritualised form of sleep. The circular structure recalls that of an observatory, while the raised couches also suggest sarcophagi. Beneath and inside each pedestal is a chamber in which a magic lantern show is projected over something resembling a hospital bed. Above and facing outwards is a form of sleep in the universal with evocations of the dreams of the dead. Below and facing inwards are the manifestations of delusion, medicalised, narcotised and maybe pathological. The most important component in the installation is intangible and elusive and yet more powerful than its material counterpoint. It makes complete sense that Ilya should understand his working methods in terms of primary and secondary forms of composition. Many of his works have a narrative element, particularly the albums where the visual focus is qualified by a literary elaboration, but also many of the installations which involve the viewer in a sequence of movements and reflections. Despite this, the initial germ of each new phase of work, in what he describes as a daily practice, is a visual idea that becomes the basis of a 'virtual tour in the head'. Grasping the size of the work and refining its detail is consigned almost entirely to the business of mental preparation, so that the actual, physical realisation of the work is regarded as little more than a 'reproduction' of the work already finished in the head. This prodigious investment in the work of the imagination, rather than of the hand or the eye in their engagement with matter, has deep roots in the experience of a samizhdat culture. Ilya compares it to the process of preparing to make a film. Now transplanted to the eastern seaboard of the United States, he sits in front of a novelty version of a Hollywood clapper-board, inscribed impishly but tellingly with the following legends: 'Production: SO-VART / Direction: Kabakov / Camera: Kabakov.' Soviet Art is not only the subject matter of the Kabakovs' work and the source of its inspiration, it also projects what many Russians and Eastern Europeans still carry round in their heads and live through on a daily basis, whatever the material changes in the world around them.

2005

A Perfect Likeness

There are three versions of Michelangelo's *David* to which people flock continuously. The first is the original, now in the Accademia in Florence; the second is the copy standing in the Piazza Signoria in the same city; and the third is one of dozens of casts in the Cast Courts of the V&A. The first is the right statue in the wrong place, having been abstracted from the vital centre of Florence's civic reality and installed in the focal position in a temple to art; the closer you get to the *David*, the less crowded the rooms become, until the point is reached where the competition has melted away altogether and you are left to contemplate a single sculpture, enshrined by the domed chamber it inhabits. The only context which the Accademia lends to *David* is that of Art. The second of these three figures is the wrong statue in the right place. It looks slightly hunkier, despite the difficulty of holding its own against the backdrop of a large Palazzo, where it stands guard like a bouncer, eying the nearby loggia with its gang of later and lesser works. But it carries art into the social setting of a large Italian city which refined the idea and practice of citizenship through its use of public space. When you walk around this *David* you are drawing it into the context of a social and political culture worth having but now mostly lost. You might think that the third figure is simply the wrong statue in the wrong place. But, in fact, this judgement might be wrong on both counts. The V&A's *David* is the epitome of the work of art in an era of mechanical reproduction, set in the frame of the history of the modern museum, which is where most of us now come to terms with the role and meanings of art.

More than any other nineteenth-century institution, the V&A brought modernity into the museum. Its collections started by amalgamating two quite disparate groups of objects: the collection of plaster casts used for teaching in the London School of Design (founded in 1837), and the residue of the huge number of manufactured items assembled for the Great Exhibition of 1851. This was a strange but entirely appropriate collaboration between the art of industry and the industrialisation of art. The multiplication of versions of the same work of art gave an association of the production line to an activity that most people had learned to value, and even venerate, in terms of uniqueness and originality; the greatest artists were thought of as 'inimitable'. But sculpture had always been different from painting, literature and music, in this respect. The traditions of classical sculpture had been absorbed almost entirely through imitations. Before the Elgin marbles were shown in London, few people in Britain had experienced Greek sculpture unless in the form of Graeco-Roman copies. Exhibition practice throughout the nineteenth century depended on the availability of casts. When Henry Cole brokered the convention of 1867 by which fifteen European states agreed to contribute sculpture to a series of circulating exhibitions, none of them envisaged lending anything but reproductions. Methods of display seemed to enforce the connection with manufacturing and commerce through an enthusiasm for overcrowding that made some galleries resemble warehouses. Surviving cast courts retain this look of the depository. The Accademia provides a case in point, with its long lines of nineteenth-century casts filling all the available space. The Cast Courts at the V&A have more character than this; although both rooms are visually very busy, their juxtapositions are unpredictable and revealing.

There is an important sense in which casts are more authentic than copies, not to mention fakes, of which a large number entered all the major museums, including the V&A, during the nineteenth century. The mania for casts turned it into a more expensive and laborious means of satisfying the same impulse behind the mid-century vogue for photography. Those who could afford it, had their offspring photographed, but those who could afford a lot more, had bits of their babies cast in three-dimensional form. The resulting collections of monumentalised tiny hands and feet make for strange viewing. Perhaps the most surreal is the array of miniature royal body parts now on show at Osborne House in the Isle of Wight. But this sentimentalising of a culture of mimicry touches on an aspect of casting that is specific to its condition: its relation to cultural memory. Casts, like photographs, capture a moment in the life of an object whose material form continues to undergo change, often imperceptibly, but sometimes quite dramatically. The great collection of casts in the Museum of Classical Archaeology in Cambridge preserves the nineteenth-century condition of many archaic bas-reliefs whose originals have deteriorated quite significantly in the smog-laden Attica of the twentieth century.

The ratio of preservation and loss, of memory and forgetfulness, is one of the most powerful themes in contemporary art, nowhere more so than in the sculpture of Rachel Whiteread. Her work in the East Court provides a particularly strong focus on the use of casting as a materialisation of memory. Its faithful record of a non-descript room holds its own in the company of the Pisano pulpit and Trajan's Column. The two bays of the original space have been reversed into two buttresses that together form a kind of propylaeon, turning a pair of blunt cul-de-sacs into the shape of a grand entrance. The room was occupied by George Orwell during his employment by the BBC, and the conceptual link this enables is with the imaginatively daunting interior of Room 101, as described in 1984. Room 101 was the locus of memory correction, the place where insidious manipulation of historical memory is transformed joltingly into the traumatic revision of a personal sense of self. That scenario is unseen and unheard, except for the nagging anomaly of a break in the seal, a tiny aperture that links inside and outside, obverse and reverse, original and copy. All plaster casts have these somewhere. In Whiteread's work, it is one of the windows that is imperfectly closed, open just enough for a sound to escape, at least in the imagination. The cast is a figure for the way art changes its meanings in the course of history. Its real original is not an object in space but a moment in time. Whiteread shows this brilliantly. Her flat surfaces are ribbed, which means pitted, with various unfathomable scars, but the most individuating details of all are supplied by that most ubiquitous and most effacing of substances, filler, the very thing designed to be invisible. Its presence here as reminder of something we are clearly supposed to forget invites us to reflect on the scope of casts in the cultural history of the West.

2006

Not Him

The title of the exhibition now running at the Royal Hibernian Academy in Dublin is 'I not I', which proposes a symmetry non-existent in the Beckett title it is alluding to. The show is organised around filmed versions of three Beckett texts (*Breath*, *Act Without Words* I and *Not I*) and features both direct responses to Beckett's work, and imagined associations with it, in videos and sculptures by Bruce

Nauman and canvases by Philip Guston. It may be that the assertive doubling of the first person pronoun is intended to emphasise the curator's desire to find resilience rather than defeat in Beckett's work, even in texts where these qualities and outcomes are held in unbearable tension. The real gamble of this exhibition involves the encircling of three distinct interpretations of Beckett's work with the parallel enquiries of Guston and Nauman in order to 'offer some companionship' to the writer's vision. Companionship, or at least 'company' of some sort, is often hinted at in Beckett's post-war oeuvre, but it is effectively fended off in Neil Jordan's filmed version of Not I (2000). Apart from a few seconds at the start of the film, the camera stays glued to a close-up examination of the mouth of the actress Julianne Moore. This makes it impossible for the viewer to be aware of the mysterious 'auditor' present in the stage productions. In Beckett's original conception, the mouth was faintly lit within a large area of surrounding darkness, with none of the rest of the face or body visible. In Jordan's version, the actress walks into view fully lit and sits down in a seat with headrest and armrests that look like they have been designed for restraint. From then on, the focus stays on the bright Hollywood perfection of Moore's lips and gleaming teeth, which form a curious barrier to identification in the experiencing of a text that pivots on questions of identification: suspending it, leading towards it, hesitating it. Beckett's 'Mouth' cannot keep company with herself, but is pushed to the brink of doing so, and the audience is meant to accompany her in this struggle. Not I and Act Without Words I are among Beckett's most Sisyphean works, but on the page they seem to keep in balance the opposing forces of prohibition and resurgence, the reasons for 'not going on' and 'going on' simultaneously. Karel Reisz's filmed version of Act Without Words I (2000) tips the balance in favour of prohibition, converting neutral stage directions into facial expressions of despair and chagrin. Strangely enough, it is in Damien Hirst's account of Breath (2000), perhaps the most reductive text in the entire oeuvre, that the spirit of resurgence is reflected. The static point of view of a theatre audience is replaced by the dramatically mobile vector of a camera in orbit over the tableau of rubbish, with at least the suggestion of a diurnal rhythm of renewal.

Of the two artists whose work is juxtaposed with these three versions of Beckett's vision, Nauman is the more direct in his response to the writer's example. The earliest of his films and videos being screened, Slow Angle Walk (1968), is actually subtitled 'Beckett Walk'. The later compositions, Good Boy, Bad Boy (1985) and Clown Torture (1987) are much more ambitious in conception, and provide lurid magnifications of typically Beckettian scenarios, but their tone and address are much more brutal and less complicated than anything in Beckett's prose or drama. Clown Torture focuses on apparently endless repetitions or prolongations of the same kind of hopeless Sisyphean impasse, without any glimmer of alleviation or any approximation to Beckett's use of humour. This spectacle of endurance is one of several Nauman works in which the experience of the viewer is one of mild torment. With Good Boy, Bad Boy, the antagonism is pronounced; the address to the audience is full-frontal and increasingly aggressive. In Beckett's texts, the relationship between speaker and reader or listener is often managed with sarcastic wit, not with splenetic confrontation. Guston's mordancy seems more Beckettian than Nauman's angry futility. His use of cartoon-like figuration has an edge of humour equivalent to Beckett's use of sarcasm to encrypt trauma and catastrophe. Interestingly, the images on display include that of Aggressor (1978) which bears a superficial resemblance to Nauman's scenarios of confrontation. However, the two figures in this painting oppose one another literally eyeball to eyeball, with an absurdity that recalls the mirroring, doubling and symbiosis that Beckett renders so poignantly throughout his oeuvre. In the end, it is a closely similar variety of tones, ranging from the deadly to the ludicrous, that Guston and Beckett seem to share – that Nauman's more schematic portrayals of alienation seem powerless to reflect.

2006

Birth of a Mountain

'I am standing on the summit of Berlin, a mountain of rubble two miles long and four hundred feet high.' The words are not taken from an account of the city's destruction in 1945, nor from a dystopian fiction of the future, but from a journal entry for the 20 November 2006. The huge massif of the city-mound is known as Teufelsberg, 'the devil's mountain', and is only one – by far the largest – of a dozen artificial hills created after 1945 to enclose the ruins of the historic centre, eighteen million cubic metres of it. In the sixty or more years since work began, entire forests have advanced from Grunewald to colonise its slopes, now quartered by wild boar and joggers with hunting dogs. At the highest point, still shut in behind a double wire fence, is the Cold War radar station, the outer skin of its main tower now pocked and torn, a flimsy canvas cladding dropping away from a steel trellis. Anything more substantial might break up when the underlying clinker starts to shift and subside. As it seems to do in the last two hundred metres of the ascent – loose bricks, Belgian blocks and shattered stones slide underfoot where the soil has been washed downhill. A weathered placard flaps in the wind, arguing that the site has been reserved for development as a 're- sort', planned to open in 2002: a project long since shelved. To the north-east of the main summit is a slightly lower, table-topped slag heap where groups of men gather with fighting dogs.

The rubble mountain sits, like a Middle Eastern *Tel*, sev- eral kilometres from the city centre. And yet this is now the physical location for much of historic Berlin. Mean- while, in the geographical centre, there are still large areas of empty land undergoing sporadic development. On Zim- merstrasse, near a waste lot the size of a country field, with meadow grasses and saplings up to six feet tall, a hot air balloon representing the corporate emblem for Die Welt is tethered and hesitating. It does not fly on windy days, ac- cording to a measurement that disqualifies nine days out of ten. Which may be why Zeppelin have diversified into the titanic concrete weights used as ballast for high-rise cranes, which are ubiquitous. Ubiquitous also the tall yellow cylin- ders filled with cement that have become an important el- ement in the city's architecture, seen to best effect opposite the Polish Apothecary's on Friedrichstrasse. They already seem more permanent than brick and stone. As you walk south towards the source of ambiguous winter daylight, passing a ham-fisted old man, in the squared shoulders of a communist-era leather jacket, pummelling his mobile phone, everything starts to look temporary. All the outside museums – museums to the history of the Berlin Wall, to the Nuremberg trials, to the 'Topography of Terror' – all are mounted on temporary structures. The city of disposable buildings is speeding up its replacement cycle. Even the new Hauptbahnhof has been closed temporarily after nuts and bolts started to fall out of its cranial vault.

The city centre, no man's land for much of the post-war period, is now a vortex of clearances, displacements – a mechanism for the conversion of waste. Close to the fiercely transformed area of the Potsdamer Platz is the Martin-Gropius-Bau, now housing a major exhibition of the works of Rebecca Horn. Right at the centre of the building, right at the conceptual centre of the show, is the monumental new commission, 'Birth of a Pearl'. This is a highly stylised arrangement of lenses and containers that represents a gigantic filtration system, reminiscent of the conditions that allow for the creation of a pearl, starting from an irritation that consolidates waste at the very centre of an organism. Both this installation and the exhibition as a whole insist on radial action and radial organisation as their most obsessive principles of construction. There are a couple of rooms devoted to the props and photographic records of long extinguished performances – blueprints anticipating something lost in the past, dusty masks and abandoned stage costumes in a performance morgue. The kinetic sculptures, which first alerted me to the strange, unsettling brilliance of Horn's work, are mostly switched off. And this presents the opportunity to focus on the series of large crayon drawings, vividly full of movement, like energy graphs, sections through the vortex that show both whirling intensity and geometrical control. 'Blau in Zwischenzustand' (pen, pencil, acrylic and Indian ink on paper) is a good example of this genre, the two-dimensional evocation of an entire hemisphere of simultaneous but various trajectories, ballistic flight-paths bending the laws of gravity. The drawings are like blueprints for the creation of a planet, a surplus of flying particles beginning to acquire a sense of the atmosphere that forms around an absent sphere. Like the pearl contraption, these diagrams are all about waste, not as a residue that is extruded or dispersed, but as a resource that is polarised, focused on, the act of concentration on waste becoming the most vital activity of art and indeed its very reason for being. Perhaps the most poignant of all the exhibits is the arrangement of 'Wounded Stones', boulder fragments stranded on vertical planes like the art-house equivalents of broken erratics, left after the departure of pigmented glaciers.

Meanwhile, closer to the Reichstag and the Brandenburg Gate, in the new Akademie der Künst, the Hans Haacke retrospective is dominated by the equipment needed for the recreation of Haacke's 1969 installation, 'Constellation'. This is a vast hydraulic system, laid out on the floor, using hundreds of metres of thin transparent tubing to make visible the kind of capillary action that makes cell-building possible in plants. Unlike its organic equivalent, Haacke's circulatory system is a closed network. (Plants can breathe.) However many junctions there are creating fission and divergence, there are just as many equivalent junctions ensuring fusion and convergence. The mechanism pumps out waste, but ends up pumping it in again. There is nowhere else to go; and in this, the Haacke installation, surrounded by documentation of less abstract, more overtly politicised interventions in the representation of German history and German identity, offers a powerful counterpoint to Horn's tension between centre and periphery. The history of the city has revolved around fission and fusion from the start; it was formed initially from the fusion of two townships, Berlin and Koln, and the subsequent centuries of rivalry between the citizenry and its rulers have seen repeated attempts at building walls of unification, and walls of division, that have all been destroyed, and their materials reclaimed or displaced; history is something repeatedly disposed of, but never entirely obliterated – in fact, the higher the mound of rejectamenta, the more it blocks out the view of anything else.

The Fifth Book of Alfred Doblin's *Berlin Alexanderplatz* revolves around the tearing up of the city fabric to make way for the extension of the transport network. Much of the description of this feverish activity in the mid-1920s fits the situation around the Alexanderplatz today. Doblin is particularly fascinated by the mounds of rubble:

A dump-heap lies before us. Dust thou art, to dust returnest. We have built a splendid house, nobody comes in or goes out any longer. Thus Rome, Babylon, Nineveh, Hannibal, Caesar, all went to smash, oh, think of it! In the first place, I must remark they are digging those cities up again, as the illustrations in last Sunday's edition show, and, in the second place, those cities have fulfilled their purpose, and we can now build new cities. Do you cry about your old trousers when they are mouldy and rotten? No, you simply buy new ones, that keeps the world going.

The historical irony in this politics and aesthetics of replacement, is that a large inscription quoting from Doblin's fifth book can still be seen on the East German apartment block adjacent to the Alexanderplatz, which has just been face-lifted out of all recognition. There is even talk of removing the inscription. Former East Germans are unnerved with the rapidity with which the material conditions of their own history, their own life-experience, are being summarily disposed of. Doubly ironic is the extent to which the East is being westernised and vice versa. During the 1980s, when I stopped off in the city en route from Poland, I acquired the habit of staying at the Kanthotel. Kantstrasse, once a showcase for West German prosperity, now has more than its fair share of charity shops and vacated premises. The junction with Wilmersdorferstrasse is now an emporium for bargain basement outfitters, while the grade A designer labels have migrated to the East.

Economic and cultural value move backwards and forwards between West and East and centre and periphery, and with each move there is a curious pulse of capillary action, a pushing away that only reinforces movement around the network. History looks like a system of aversions, epitomised in the popularity of the East German allotment system. These are allotments entirely without plants, only neat prefabricated chalets all angled away from each other in an endless series of mutual exclusions. In the floods of pearly light below the smog incised by the East German TV tower, they seem to go on for ever.

Ordungsamt

In the flea-markets of the Ostbahnhof, the Arkonaplatz and the Mauer-Park, you can see the demise of a culture putting into frenzied circulation a hoard of objects held close for decades, now magically obsolete, objects of nostalgia, parody, dislocation: the artefactual evidence of life in the DDR. The markets are well attended; crowds of Berliners make their way silently along the tram routes and the unterbahns, moving nervously from one venue to another. After a while, the habitués are easy to spot, especially the tall, spindly eccentric with his short, stout companion, looking like Don Quixote and Sancho Panza, both dressed in olive green military oilskins with field belts and webbing, standing out from the rest of the Cold War-demob wanderers as they pick their way through four different markets in as many hours. They are not buying or selling anything – apart from the occasional beer – but have come to preside over the drowning of a generation, all going down for the third time with their entire lives flashing before their eyes.

In the original flea markets, infected garments were bought for reluctant use, but the goods on sale here are all for eye-level shelving, rescued from previously ignorable backgrounds of daily life in order to be thrust into the foreground of an elegiac sense of vanishing waymarks – of the sudden, keenly felt absence of mislaid and abandoned mementoes, once so familiar (contemptibly familiar) but now recalled with a slightly disturbing fondness, the kind of fondness only objects can lay claim to; trusty in a world without trust; they are things that define a home, though they could be found in anyone's home; household gods in an age of mechanical reproduction; each and every one the banal locus of an indefinable ache.

The tightly packed stalls are a distillation without taxonomy, offering an experience overcrowded with recollections as incongruous as in a dream. The markets are obsessional walkways, corridors between past and future, and have sprung up in close proximity to the former course of the Berlin Wall, which was not only a physical separation but a temporal barrier between alternative pasts and futures. The Checkpoint Charlie museum is now for tourists, but Berliners themselves keep coming back at the weekends to these pop-up frontiers of the memory that call for urgent patrolling, watching and checking for escape attempts, for the furtive manoeuvres of a mindset still at odds with itself, with its own inveterate yearnings: no freedom without order; no cure for the soul without paying, over and over again, to take back something of what was lost, in the blackmail of self that is recent German history.

2007

'Light': A Total Installation

The setting for this exhibition is infused not only with the exact ratio of light and shade predominant on any given day, but with more than nine hundred years of thinking about the meaning of light in sacred space. The history of architecture attributes the birth of Gothic to the reconstruction of the east end of the Abbey of Saint-Denis in 1144, when Abbot Suger authorised a design that transformed the relationship between church architecture and light. His innovation was the creation of a 'crown of chapels, because of which the entire church would brilliantly shine with the remarkable and uninterrupted light of the dazzling windows illuminating the interior beauty'. A century and a half later, William Durandus wrote his *Rationale Divinorum Officiorum* (1286), the most influential of all medieval treatises on the symbolic meaning of churches and church ornaments. This codifies the importance of light in the Gothic cathedral, and accounts for the symbolic meaning of its physical presence there: 'the glass windows in a church are Holy Scriptures, which expel the wind and the rain, that is all things hurtful, but transmit the light of the true Sun, that is God, into the hearts of the faithful. These are wider within than without, because the mystical sense is the more ample, and precedes the literal meaning.' Written in the late thirteenth century, Durandus's text is effectively a practical manual for churchmen, but it is based on ideas whose most sophisticated philosophical treatment had been given in the text *De Luce*, written by the Englishman Robert Grosseteste around the time of the rebuilding of Saint-Denis.

We think of light as intangible, without substance, and yet, according to Grosseteste, it is 'the first corporeal form', the very means by which matter comes into being and takes on form: 'for the form cannot desert matter, because it is inseparable from it, and matter itself cannot be deprived of form'. No wonder light features in the history of art as a creative force, associated more with spirit than with matter, seeming to come from a source beyond the world of objects that it reveals. Grosseteste has an explanation for the unique status of light in our perception and understanding of the world: 'the first corporeal form is [...] more exalted and of a nobler and more excellent essence than all the forms that come after it [...] It has moreover greater similarity than all bodies to the forms that exist apart from matter, namely, the intelligences.'

Light is undoubtedly a part of the physical world and yet it seems to enter the world through divine or angelic agency. This is one reason why the medieval builders sought to use light as an element of architecture in the great cathedrals. At Winchester, the cathedral encompasses both Romanesque and Gothic building styles and exemplifies the architectural importance of light in the design of its arcades, galleries and clerestories and in its use of stained glass. Light is a malleable medium that can be channelled, relayed, absorbed, reflected and refracted. Pilar Beltran Lahoz's 'Container' provides perhaps the purest expression of the architectural manipulation of light. It has the geometrical simplicity and the scale of the kind of rectangular box we normally identify with industrial containers, and its fabric is imprinted faintly with the details of just such a container, and yet it is designed to contain nothing; or rather, it contains nothing but light and air. To be strictly accurate, it both does and does not contain light, since its use of silkscreen materials transforms light into denser and more obscure forms, while its visual permeability does not stop light in its tracks – does not prevent it from travelling into and out of the space delineated by its aluminum frames. The architectural use of silk – the least substantial and most gossamer-like of materials – invites the imagination to regard the work of art as both a visual and a tactile experience, since silk is normally worn on the body, close to the skin. It uses our knowledge of silk to convey the delicacy and unresisting quality of the threshold between greater and lesser degrees of clarity and obscurity, a relationship that is usually negotiated in medieval cathedrals through the medium of stained glass. The chiaroscuro effect dramatises the relationship that light always seems to evoke, between the material and immaterial, between the spirit and its fleshly envelope.

The same fragility in the separation of these conditions, that are conventionally regarded as opposite, but which light seems to blend, is clearly at the centre of Marc Quinn's remarkable 'Angel'. Based on the cast of a foetal skeleton, Quinn's tiny figure is a reminder of the basic liminality of the human condition. Without doubt already a part of the material world, the foetus is often regarded in the modern secular imagination as only uncertainly and indeterminately a part of humanity. At the same time, the traditional religious attitude has consigned the stillborn child to limbo, as if it does not qualify somehow in spiritual terms. Quinn's conception seems to run counter to both these habits of thought. The extraordinary delicacy of the foetal organism involves a material condition so refined as to be almost spiritualised. Quinn's sculpture embodies an almost Wordsworthian attitude towards the child – that the less developed it is, the closer it is to God: that it comes to life 'trailing clouds of glory' (a phrase that you can only visualise in terms of chiaroscuro). The nineteenth-century framework for this attitude was provided by the moment of birth, but Quinn pushes back the margin as far as it will go, to the moment of conception. His title makes a claim for the idea that an embryonic condition is the most likely of all to be spiritual in nature. Resistance to this hypothesis could be strengthened by an assumption that the foetus lives in darkness, enclosed and withdrawn from the light of creation; but we now know that this is not true; that the walls of the womb and the human body act as a medium for the absorption and transmission of light and for its separation into different colours. The accession of light suggests powerfully that drawing a line between different states of being is something that humanity does subjectively, and even arbitrarily. The fact that Quinn's 'Angel' is praying in a westerly direction suggests a more urgent need to intercede with humanity than with God.

Both Lahoz and Quinn are concerned with the tenuousness of the barrier between presence and absence, almost discounting the difference between visibility and invisibility. Rachel Whiteread's untitled pair of works appears to provide a counterweight to this approach, emphasising boundedness and solidity. The architectural role of these reciprocal objects depends on the parallels and modifications they offer to the genre of the funerary monument, examples of which are found in every part of the cathedral. Their extreme plainness, their economy of signification, is echoed most fully and straightforwardly in the funerary slab of Bishop de Lucy, which occupies an equivalent position at the other end of the cathedral, at the east end of the retrochoir. This symmetry is an extension of the principles of organisation that govern all of Whiteread's most characteristic works, involving the production of casts of both solids and voids, presences and absences. Although the work in 'Light' is divided into two closely similar elements whose simplicity raises them almost to the level of abstraction, they are in fact representations of a solid object and of the vacancy above it, manifestations both of the material and of the immaterial, one convex and the other concave. Both are given equal value and placed in corresponding positions by the west door, like the twin bastions of an ancient propylaeon. One is the cast of a mortuary slab, effectively the plinth for a cadaver, while the other can be thought of as another kind of container for light, capturing the space from which human remains have been removed, or spirited away – representations, then of mortality and of what mortality defines itself against.

The smooth, polished whiteness of Whiteread's composition could not be further removed from the distressed complexity of the surface of John Gibbons's aptly named 'Presence'. Virtually every part of this highly concentrated work has been milled and abraded to produce a swirling, rippling pattern that entangles and confuses light. Even slight movement on the part of the viewer circling round this sculpture will trigger a release of visual energy. But energy does not merely skid across its surface; it has been recruited in a tremendous effort of containment. The welds and patches that hold this work together seem to have enclosed a source of power that presses against its confinement in a way characteristic of many of Gibbons's works. The elevation and dimensions of the work evoke the origins of monumental sculpture in many traditions, particularly the Egyptian and Greek, and the tension between abstraction and figuration recalls the compactness of expression of the Cycladic bronze age. This amalgamation of the archaic and the contemporary seems to place the work in a modernist tradition of the kind sponsored by Wilhelm Worringer in Abstraction and Empathy (1908), a text that relegated sentimental Romanticism in favour of the austere impersonality of ancient devotional art. If nineteenth-century sculpture was an art of empathy, of identification with aspects of the human condition, with impermanence and frailty, its twentieth-century successor was to focus on what exceeded individual human experience, on the kind of unknowability traditionally associated with the divine. If Gibbons's brooding stela invites any form of identification, it is of the kind associated with totemic objects that give a visual form to an unseen presence, a spirit that forms the basis simultaneously of a belief system and a social system, as if the two could not be thought of separately.

Darren Almond's 'Geisterbahn' ['Ghost Train'] is a video installation in the crypt. Ghost trains are a product of the leisure industry, and yet they have a cathartic, almost ritual function for those who ride them, suggesting a debased form of religious experience that taps into primitive anxieties and superstitions. This particular amalgam of the modern and the archaic was made possible by the Victorian technology that developed the underground train from the 1860s onwards. David L. Pike's study *Subterranean Cities* (2005) has shown how the early attempts at establishing subterranean rail networks gave birth to a cultural history that identified them with entry into an infernal realm. The Underground acquired associations with the Land of the Dead. The simultaneous projection of a modern metropolis overground and of a lair of dark spirits beneath it was contemporaneous with the development of theories of the unconscious, which allowed for the realisation that modern civilisation retains an intimate psychological relationship with primitive desires and phobias. The joining together of the technological and the pathological was characteristic of a rich vein in early cinema, particularly in German Expressionism, which Almond's film recalls in its iconography, technique and title. 'Geisterbahn' is essentially a black and white silent film with added music. Its absence of colour accentuates the basis of the film medium, which is a projection of patterns of light and shade. The obscurity of some of the images is the calculated effect of an emphasis on strong contrasts, corresponding visually to the many thematic dualities of the work.

David Batchelor's assemblage, 'Waldella 6', uses light equally as medium and as subject matter, although this is not the daylight referred to by medieval builders and theorists, but the artificial light produced in an economy that thinks of it as a resource rather than as a natural phenomenon. If Grosseteste emphasises the exalted status of light, Batchelor channels it through the least regarded of materials, the recycled bottles used previously to contain domestic cleaning substances. The siting of these mass-produced vessels, in a vertical festoon slanted downwards on one of the great piers of the south aisle, invites immediate comparison with the pattern of colours often visible on the adjacent pier. The visual array created by light percolating through stained glass is both complemented and subverted by Batchelor's spectacle in dyed plastic. The reuse of disposable materials is an ethical choice that requires adjustment of an assumed hierarchy of values. At the same time, the reference to cleaning, maintenance and economic imperatives is a reminder of the dual existence of the church as both a symbolic structure and a physical edifice implanted within a social and commercial reality. The primary colours with which the bottles have been stained draw attention to the physical basis of light in a spectrum of colours, no less than the artist requires the viewer to contemplate the meaning of sacred space in relation to a range of constituents.

Ian Dawson's convulsive blend of colours and forms, '171 Elements', seems to perform the act of creation in reverse. An extensive series of identifiable objects (chairs, crates, scooters, toys of various kinds) have been swallowed up by an expanding slick of plastic whose motion seems to have been arrested only temporarily. If medieval thought is fixated on light as the outcome of the first act of creation, as the means of introducing form into the world, Dawson proposes the secondary act of creation, the activity of artists, as a means of devolving form, of returning differentiated objects to an original state of potential. In this respect, his giant synthetic blastoma provides a challenging counterpoint to the highly specific development of Quinn's foetal sculpture in the opposite aisle. Dawson has taken the evidence of modern everyday life in its most familiar and undervalued aspects and melted it down in a utopian gesture that suggests the possibility for reforming it in quite literal as well as metaphorical ways. Its ambivalence is such that it could represent the point at which light begins to disappear from the world, its separate colours on the point of muddied convergence, or it could stand for the hope that would accompany a second creation, the birth of new forms in the light of the artistic imagination.

2007

Margaret Tait
Selected Films 1952–1976 (Lux, 2006);
Subjects and Sequences: A Margaret Tait Reader,
ed. Peter Todd and Benjamin Cook (Lux, 2004)

Margaret Tait has made little impact on the cultural history of twentieth-century Britain, and yet her varied output of films, photographs, poems and stories is both distinguished and compelling. Born in Orkney in 1918, she later went to school and university in Edinburgh, served in the Royal Army Medical Corps from 1943 to 1946, studied film at the Centro Sperimentale di Cinematografia in Rome between 1950 and 1952, and founded her own production company, Ancona Films, in 1953. From 1954 she was living and working in Rose Street, Edinburgh, returning finally to the 'windy Orkney isles' as she calls them in A Portrait of Ga – her affectionate short film about her mother – for perhaps the most productive phase of her career between 1968 and her death in 1999. Since her death, a selection of her films and writings has begun to circulate in the public domain, thanks mainly to the restoration and editing work sponsored by the Lux organisation.

Tait made only one feature film, and the greater part of her oeuvre shows little interest in narrative or character, focusing rather on the observation of everyday life and especially on the environs of her workplaces in Edinburgh and Orkney. Although learning a great deal from the Italian neorealist tradition and evoking often the preoccupations of the British documentary movement, Tait never uses film as a medium for the transfer of information. The sound consists of snatches of music or recordings of ambient noise; the speaking voice is seldom heard, and when it is, is often pushed into background indistinctness. The imagery is circular, with the same motifs reappearing in several works, yet always held in place quite specifically on each occasion. What separates one work from the next in the viewer's mind is the fundamental but elusive experience of rhythm and structure.

This structural emphasis takes a form that is found only rarely in film but which is familiar to readers of poetry. It is indicative that the recent selection of Tait's writings published by Lux has been given the title Subjects and Sequences. The poetic sequence offers the closest parallel to the way several of Tait's longer compositions are segmented, with each component section often being given its own title.

The modular structure both relieves and sharpens concentration. Within each section, the camera dwells on a chosen area, indoors or outdoors, often with only slight or gradual movement. The measure and pace are contemplative, which has the effect of transferring the responsibility of primary attention from filmmaker to viewer. Clearly, Tait is the one who has chosen the subject matter and who has positioned the camera, but the scope given to the individual viewer for a subjective exploration of each scene is pivotal; it reflects the kind of experience of a particular place in all its granularity that is simultaneously an experience of time. What one learns from these films is a rhythm of attention, a way of inhabiting duration that seems to be dictated more by the setting than by the intentions of the filmmaker. This is so much the case that when the shadow of Tait holding the camera comes into shot, as it does in *Place of Work* (1976), or when her reflection is seen in a mirror, as it is in *Tailpiece* (1976), the effect is one of intrusion and shock.

The use of measure in poetry is one of the chief means by which it relates to convention, intersects with tradition, and there is a similar yielding to the pressure of history in Tait's work. For the filmmaker, the customary rhythms of work and play, the ceremonies of relationship marking the arrangements of days, weeks, years, provide the structure both of individual lives and of communities. John Grierson wrote of the necessity for the documentary filmmaker to identify and record those gestures that 'time has worn smooth' in order to capture the experience of communities bound together in time as well as space. Tait scrutinises gesture in a similar way, but while she searches out those gestures that already have a history, she also composes gestures that evoke one. This aspect of her work is perhaps most striking in her 1964 portrait of the poet Hugh

MacDiarmid. The film conveys very little about the subject matter of MacDiarmid's poetry, or the international range of his intellectual and cultural concerns; there is no indication of the significance of his socialism, or of his commitment to Scottish nationalism; there is only very sparse quotation of the poet's own words. In place of all this, MacDiarmid is seen engrossed in conversation in an Edinburgh pub, or observed in the course of reading or writing, immersed in his daily routines; but most of all, he is seen performing a gesture that seems eccentric and whimsical at first, but which is also deeply satisfying as a reflection of his artistic modus operandi. His slight figure is seen stepping precariously along the kerbstones of Edinburgh, waving his arms to keep balance as if walking the tightrope, smiling but also frowning with concentration. This playful manoeuvre epitomises a lifetime of showing off, of confident risk-taking, of intellectual coordination and artistic agility. There is a related scene in which the linguistically amphibious MacDiarmid walks down some quayside steps to the water's edge, advancing and retreating with sudden movements to avoid wetting his feet. These precisely choreographed gestures capture the poet's impulse towards brinkmanship, which one can imagine him performing as a child as well as at the age of seventy-one.

Twelve years earlier, in 1952, Tait had composed a similar sequence of steps for her mother to perform in a country lane, a pensioner skipping like a young girl in the sunlit Orkney landscape. The economy of this image, which uses a single figure to suggest continuity between generations, seems somehow sharper in an island context, since islands in their boundedness provide a more intense focus on inherited practices and rituals, on customs in common. But the most unforgettable image in the film, one of the most arresting moments in Tait's oeuvre, is that of her mother's fingers unwrapping a sticky boiled sweet. This extraordinary performance, determined and painstaking, but also balletic and graceful, seems to sum up a lifetime of patience, resourcefulness and aesthetic tact that seems rooted both in personality and in a shared history.

2007

The Real Avant-Garde

I first walked into Kettle's Yard shortly after arrival in Cambridge in 1973. I had come to study English and to try to write. For me – as for anyone concerned with experimental art – the house by the church gave spatial form to an historical problem. You could say it enshrined the paradox of the twentieth-century avant-gardes: the pursuit of new forms, the discovery of organising principles specific to the medium, and the vexed question of how these formalist goals relate to the society that has produced them. In Kettle's Yard, the question of how we actually live with experimental art was given practical form – and a very English character – in Jim Ede's arrangements, but the full scope of the question has been addressed and readdressed in a series of temporary exhibitions. To my mind, the value of these exhibitions was epitomised in the Polish Constructivism show of 1984. This was typically farsighted, bringing Polish Constructivist paintings, sculptures and publications to Britain for the first time, and typically overarching, exhibition and catalogue together encapsulating an entire history of debate around issues echoed in the more familiar wrangles of western art movements.

Polish Constructivism between the mid-1920s and the late 1930s was essentially a series of arguments about the relationship between art and twentieth-century production processes. There were three overlapping phases, each associated with different artistic groupings and group publications. The first, *Blok*, was the earliest and most short-lived, initiated in 1924 and succeeded in 1926 by *Praesens*, which lasted until 1939, despite a major change of direction and of personnel. Both of these movements involved collaboration and rivalry between artists and architects. The distinguishing feature of the third phase, which led to the formation of a group calling itself *a.r.*, was a series of joint projects involving both artists and writers. The initial letters *a.r.* stood alternatively for *awangarda rzeczywista* [the real avant-garde] and for *arstysci rewolucyjni* [revolutionary artists]. The obvious protagonist in each of these three scenarios was Wladyslaw Strzeminski, the most radical formalist in the history of Polish Constructivist painting, and the busiest controversialist. The reason *Blok* was so short-lived was intransigence on the part of both Strzeminski and Mieczyslaw Szczuka, who clashed over the theoretical subordination of art to questions of social utility. Szczuka wished to place art at the service of town-planning and industrial design, while Strzeminski believed in its independence from existing forms of urbanism as the basis for imagining entirely different social structures in the future. *Praesens* started harmoniously with the idea of promoting collaborations between artists and architects, seizing opportunities to impose abstract painted designs on existing buildings, and to interpose abstract sculptures in the spaces between buildings. However, after three years, Strzeminski left the group, together with the painter Henryk Stazewski and the sculptor Katarzyna Kobro, convinced of the need to replace these partial measures with a unified programme of urban design, where the emphasis was on the composition of the entire architectural environment according to the same principles. During the 1930s, Strzeminski pursued the goals of *a.r.* through the much narrower focus of typographical design, with remarkable results. His settings of the poems of Julian Przybos regarded the entire page as a unified field in which the various interrelated elements were of equal significance. By these means, the visual structure could be equal in importance to the aural structure.

After seeing the relevant works in the Kettle's Yard exhibition, I was offered a job soon afterwards that would put them close to the centre of my life for the next three years. In October 1984, I went to a Readership at the University of Lodz in Poland. Lodz is home to many things: the site of the second largest Jewish ghetto; the Polish film school; an extraordinarily unified nineteenth-century architectural heritage; the Museum of Modern Art. The latter was the source of practically all the works in the Kettle's Yard Exhibition. Here they made sense not only in the context of the history of the European avant-gardes, but in terms of local buildings, murals, applied art of various kinds, and in their influence on the stubborn formalism of post-war experiments in various media, particularly film. Strzeminski had taught in local schools and the results were widespread, affecting the practice of various crafts, especially textiles. If the official art of the communist era was socialist realism, it seemed that Constructivist principles were more immanent, less declamatory but more pervasive, less aggressive but more tenacious. I was impressed by the extent to which radical abstraction could be deployed as effective resistance to a dominant ideology. It deepened my respect for Strzeminski, for the consistency and coherence of his practice, and my curiosity about, and acclimatisation to his work led to cooperation with Jozef Robakowski and Jarek Jedlinski, whose film about the painter appeared in 1993.

I prepared the text for the English version of this, and provided the voice-over for the soundtrack. But although Strzeminski had been the driving force behind the conceptual integrity of Polish Constructivism, the most beguiling objects that it ever produced were the sculptures of Kobro, which I had seen for the first time in Castle Street. Over three years, I got to know them well and to appreciate the scope of Kobro's remark 'sculpture is a part of the space around it'. The positioning of the work, physically, socially, culturally, was an unignorable element in its reception. When the Polish art collective *fabs* asked me in 2000 for a statement of compositional practice, I began with Kobro's dictum, believing that it could reflect my sense of how I wanted the poetic text to relate to the different languages that surround it. But the debt was acknowledged in more suitable form in 1998, when the Museum of Modern Art published my poetic sequence 'Kobro' to coincide with a major retrospective exhibition there.

Part of the debt is owing to Kettle's Yard for introducing me to all of this. The point is not the coincidence of those works being exhibited in the very year that I was contemplating a move to Poland. The point is that Kettle's Yard is the kind of space in which those kinds of works will be shown. If the idea that sculpture is a part of the space around it is not actually inscribed on the lintel, it is implied equally by the dispositions of the house and by the exhibition programme of the gallery space. It is an idea whose true scope should never be underestimated.

2007

Sutton Hoo
The Shipping Forecast

The correct approach to Sutton Hoo is from the river. The larger mounds on the ridge above the east bank of the Deben were designed to be seen from ships nosing up the channel after their journey from Sweden. Suffolk and Sweden were the only places in Europe where ship-burial was practised around the year AD 600. At Sutton Hoo, the ship-biers were dragged from ten feet above sea level to an elevation of one hundred feet in less than half a mile. The gut-wrenching effort is our best measure of East Anglian stubbornness at a time when pagan burial customs were being replaced by Christian funerary rites in other parts of the country. Two of the mounds at Sutton Hoo contained ships. The larger of the two was over ninety feet long and contained the richest grave goods ever found in Britain. The historical records for this period are scant and retrospective, and there is nothing conclusive in what was dug up to identify the occupant of Mound 1, although it is reasonable to suppose he was a Wuffing (the name given to all the East Anglian kings). The most popular nominee has always been Raedwald, who was king from 599 to 625. His name was put forward by the Cambridge scholar Hector Chadwick, who visited the first excavation in 1939, and the Raedwald idea has stuck ever since, partly, one suspects, because more is known about Raedwald than the other candidates, and what is known makes a good story. The historical evidence is incomplete, the art historical evidence allows for an earlier date, the carbon dating allows for both earlier and later dates, and the most promising dating equipment, a bag of Frankish coins, was assigned initially to c. 650; the subsequent back-dating, carried out in 1960, was jiggled, rather remarkably, to 625 precisely.

But it does not matter whether they pushed the boat out – or rather in – for Raedwald, or for some other Frankish coin collector, since the culture, a culture in every sense on the move, would have been the same. The culture presided over by Raedwald was schizoid; history shows that the direction it moved in was towards us, towards what we think of as English; but the direction it moved away from was equally English, and very different.

Bede tells us in passing that Raedwald converted to Christianity on a visit to Kent, the first of the English kingdoms to import the new faith, but got such a frosty reception on his return home, it convinced him to erect a new temple with altars both to Jesus Christ and the Devil. He gets the approval of Bede, however, for his obligingness in the story of King Edwin's conversion. Edwin was a Northumbrian royal on the run from his vindictive brother-in-law Ethelfrid; Raedwald provided a safe house, but took a serious interest in selling one Northumbrian to another before his wife intervened and introduced him to the concept of honour. Edwin's survival fulfilled the prediction of a mysterious supernatural agent who expected and obtained his conversion just for being right; Raedwald's action helped to realise a providential pattern, an important one that resulted in Edwin becoming the Christian ruler of everywhere south of the Humber. But it did not revive Raedwald's own flagging interest in the new religion; and the wife who taught him morality – the first Ethics girl – had also rubbished the idea of changing faiths when Raedwald brought it home in his luggage from Kent. Raedwald's temple was a betting shop, and the occupant of the buried ship, or whoever made the funeral arrangements, showed a similar keen interest in gaming in the shape of a large gaming board complete with a set of whale ivory pieces. The body in Mound 1 showed up in the dig as a patch of different-coloured soil, and this physical vagueness matches the elusiveness of the body's identity. Whether Raedwald or not, there was very little in his post-mortem kit to indicate that he had staked much on the chances of a Christian afterlife: only a pair of spoons, inscribed 'Saulos' and 'Paulos', which might have suggested an amiable willingness to do the conversion-job properly, if it came to it, rather than a solid conviction that the first attempt had actually worked. The spoons do not figure much among all the other stuff: the famous helmet, the bundles of spears and angons, the exceptional lyre in its beaver-skin bag, the ceremonial whetstone, looking like an imperial sceptre, a pair of shoes size 7, and the largest hoard of late Roman silver from the eastern Mediterranean ever found in northern Europe. And then the coins, which Philip Grierson thought were to pay the ferryman with, or rather, to pay a spectral crew to man the ship. They were all foreign, the coins, not the spectres, because they could not be anything else; there was no mint in business anywhere in England at that time – this was the last moment before the country asserted its island identity with its own currency. The different-coloured patch was no islander; his business interests and family connections were across the North Sea, out in the shipping lanes.

The Visitor Centre allows for this, but puts the case for retrospective Englishness with its final annexe, devoted to the Kingdom of East Anglia, AD 500–869. This caters to local patriotism, but also to a grander ambition that regards East Anglia as the seed-bed for a national character that gradually encroached on the rest of the available space. It is a fact that the earliest runic inscription in Old English yet discovered was found at Caistor by Norwich. It dates to the fifth century, and possibly even the fourth century, which raises the possibility of an intriguing overlap with the Roman presence. The evidence is inscribed on a foot-bone from the skeleton of a roe deer, and consists, very helpfully, of the word for roe deer, 'raihun', a detail that put a spring in the steps of a pair of Tolkien-enthusiasts who preceded me in our tour of the display cabinets. But if the self-naming object was not a caprice on the part of a visiting Belgian surrealist, and early East Anglia was like a fifth-century version of Swift's Laputa, with every Wuffing hiking around with a glossary of objects in his rucksack, we should recall that the version of English spoken by Raed-wald was the version which also evolved into Swedish, not to mention Danish, Norwegian, German and Dutch. There is a strong case for saying that Sutton Hoo does not mark the beginnings of Englishness, but its end: no money, no Christianity, and no island mentality. Whoever was buried in Mound 1 did not die in the ship, but he did live in one, conceptually, at least – his people were joined by the sea, not bounded by it.

The present-day access to the site is by car to the Vis-itor Centre, then on foot through a small, crooked ave-nue of thorn trees, onto a table land where there are acres of polythene-covered crops and a small roped-off area, which is where the mounds are. Only one of them now commands rather than solicits attention. Totally rebuilt in 1993, steep-sided and picturesque with gorse, it looks down on the others which have all slumped sideways, having lost their centres of gravity to centuries of plough-ing. Anti-glider trenches from the Second World War run across the heritage features. On a stormy spring day, larks swing across the bright windy spaces above, and there is the savour of salt in the air. The cloud anvils are pale to the west, and dark to the east. Not-Raedwald, progenitor of Not-England, no longer even darkens the soil.

2008

Shot by Both Sides

The medal as an art form is ideally suited to represent a microcosm of the world. A flat metal disc reflects the circular appearance of the globe if not its spherical form, while its reversible sides seem tailor-made for alternative, and even contrasting views of experience. The basic design of every medal thus supplies a pretext for the conceptual division that has marked the history of making and awarding these tokens of praise and blame, permitting the growth of opposite traditions either honouring recipients or else smearing intended or imagined recipients with attributions of dishonour. The structural reversibility built into the genre from the start has paved the way for the present exhibition, but the antithetical energy that runs so vividly through the exhibits has been generated by the convulsions of history, by specific reminders that there are two sides to every story. Medals can be thought of as aesthetically complex forms of name-calling, deploying both positive and negative terms, as if in line with Churchill's paradoxical statement that 'a medal glitters, but it also casts a shadow' (1941). Churchill is referring to the mixed feelings that may greet the award of a medal, not to any ambivalence in its design, but his motto serves as a formulation of the way in which examples of the genre always carry the potential for a contradiction in terms.

In the hands of Mona Hatoum, the medal is transformed into the indispensable medium for representing the double-sided character of our current ideological environment. Hatoum's medal is blank on the reverse, but her design does not need to encompass more than one side, since its depiction of the globe as a hand grenade, juxtaposed with an Arabic inscription, implies a world view that cannot be imagined without reference to its antithesis. For

those without Arabic, there is a further reversal of expect-
ed meaning in the translation of the inscription, which
does not sponsor violence but disowns it, and in doing so
offers a check to western assumptions about the distribu-
tion of honourable and dishonourable conduct in the so-
called war on terror.

Medals are conceptually Janus-faced in their relation to
history. They possess both transitory and enduring char-
acteristics, with their origins in a forgotten topicality that
art transforms into persistence. The two traditions of hon-
our and dishonour manage the relationship with history
in different ways. Medals of honour are more likely to be
conventional and stereotypical in form, paradoxically con-
signing their subjects to oblivion, while the inventiveness
and originality of many designs in the dishonour tradition
are more likely to preserve in the memory these responses
to ignominy. This is nowhere more true than in the Chap-
man brothers' medal, which provides an epitome of the
concerns reflected in their recent installation *Fucking Hell*
(2008). In both the medal and the larger project to which
it refers the theatre of war does not figure as the principal
setting for the kind of behaviour recognised and rewarded
in the medals of honour tradition, but is instead the total
environment within which both terrestrial and infernal
economies have become undivided. The world is not con-
tained within its sphere nor within the visible circumfer-
ence supplied by the shape of the medal, but extends be-
yond imaginative control in a limitless killing field whose
iconography is associated with the conflicts of different
historical periods as well as of different discursive fields:
economic, socio-political and cultural, as well as military.

The Chapman's hell is resolutely postmodern in its mix-
ing of registers and in its secularising and routinising of the
theologian's evil. Grayson Perry's 'For Faith in Shopping'

is in many ways its perfect complement, deploying a deliberately archaic style of representation, with aspects of Christian iconography that relate to an historical period when devotional art was, practically speaking, universal in its control of the cultural imagination, and yet substituting as the object of devotion a way of being in the world that is controlled ultimately by the power of the spectacle, no longer in the hands of fine art, but at the mercy of fashion and the media. The technologised sleekness of fashion products is clearly opposed by the palpable craftsmanship with which the worship of fashion has been modelled, giving Perry's retrograde artisanal skills the aura of authenticity in an era of virtually infinite reproducibility. Of all the works in the exhibition, his miniature tondo is the most resistant to the medal's habitual gravitation towards two dimensions; it is an anthem against flatness.

Cornelia Parker, on the other hand is an artist who has experimented enthusiastically with flattened metal in the past, sometimes flattening objects, such as brass musical instruments, whose function requires the preservation of volume. The conversion of a three-dimensional presence into a sheet of metal connoting absence signals her recognition of the extent to which the transfer of any utensil into an art context changes its meaning; the translation of its physical reality into another form is emblematic of its conceptual transformation. Parker has also made relevant use of the disc form, exploiting the ambivalence attached to the binary structure of the medal. For her *Moon Landing* project, she created a series of plaques parodying the conventions of National Trust signs, reproducing the shape and typography favoured by this organisation, but producing an effect of contrariety with the introduction of black rather than white backgrounds. This negative or alternative universe of heritage refers to an object that has been lost rather than conserved, perhaps commenting on the selective attitude towards history exemplified by heritage organisations whose interpretation of the past may displace the object of scrutiny by the manner in which they seek to retrieve it. The aversion of the two faces in Parker's medal focuses attention even more dramatically on the practice of concealment now identified with the conduct of the Iraq war, highlighting the culpability of politicians whose cover-up operations affect the making and not just the interpretation of history.

Richard Hamilton's medal seems at first glance to offer a counter-example to Parker's twin images of retraction, with its full exposure of smiling faces. However, there is an element of exaggeration in these brazen expressions, a suggestion of strain and artifice, of the erection of a facade. Hamilton is a shrewd observer of the interface between public persona and the individual whose personal motivations for public actions remain inscrutable. The element of performance in political life combines exhibitionism with concealment, requiring an almost contradictory enactment of identity, a suturing together of almost opposite tendencies; this unnatural process of collaging the self is captured brilliantly in Hamilton's well-known painting, *Portrait of Hugh Gaitskell as a Famous Monster of Filmland*, which is partly an *ad hominem* attack and partly a more general indictment of the inauthenticity of the political role, of a mode of operation in public life that resembles the condition of Frankenstein, stitched together from different versions of the self, some of which are more alien than others, grafting sincerity onto masquerade, and expediency onto conviction. The distortion of parts of the face in the portrayal of Gaitskell is echoed more subtly in the medal's characterisations of Blair and Campbell, where the careful manipulation of *bas-relief* effects literally adds a dimension to the artistic expression of Protean mutability. By moving the position of the medal, or moving one's own position in relation to it, the facial expressions of government are seen to change, to be capable of meaning more than one thing at once. Closer inspection of the milled surface reveals an unusual alternation of convexities and concavities that dramatises the chiaroscuro effects that can be achieved by more conventional modelling. Hamilton has achieved an advance in the capacity of medal-making techniques to embody alternatives and make duplicity seem ingrained, almost putting us in the position of seeing both sides at once.

The Iraq war has attracted more attention than any other scenario featured on the medals commissioned for this exhibition. The enormous media coverage it has received has turned it into a twenty-first-century theatre of cruelty, in which the testimony of sounds and images counts for more than language in any attempt to locate the evidence of honourable or dishonourable conduct. Yun-Fei Ji's medal makes a direct contrast between the hypocrisy of political rhetoric and the carnage that is performed in its name. The obverse seems to illustrate an episode in a beast fable, in which animals are given human attributes in order to make generic points about examples of folly or wisdom, moral or immoral behaviour. But in a world controlled by the interests of those embraced by the phrase 'coalition of the willing', states and their governments revert to violence in a mimicry of instinctual predation by animals. The human cost of this militarised feeding frenzy is counted on the reverse of Steve Bell's 'Collateral Damage Medal', which encapsulates the effect of the war on civilians in the single figure of a dead child. The distilled pathos of this image jars grotesquely with the monstrous image on the obverse, echoing the concealed and camouflaged heads and faces of the medals by Cornelia Parker and Richard

Hamilton. Bell's unmistakeable reference to the head of the sovereign submits the familiar image to a form of deranged swaddling, indicative of an obsessive need to see, hear, smell, taste nothing, precisely because the evidence of the senses is the only thing to be trusted after language has been corrupted by the obscene euphemisms of war.

The two remaining medals that subvert the genre's traditional iconographic focus on the portrait head are Ellen Gallagher's 'An Experiment of Unusual Opportunity' and Michael Landy's 'ASBO Medal'. The experiment referred to in Gallagher's title withheld medical treatment from American black men suffering from syphilis between 1932 and 1972 in order to collect data on the progress of the disease up to the point of death. The face of the nurse depicted on the medal is accordingly reduced to the representation of a single cyclopean eye, indicting the substitution of mere observation for the medical duty of care. The ravaged state of the neck subtended to this mutant surveillance device transfers the disease from patient to researcher in a comment on the psychological morbidity of those responsible. Michael Landy's medal is concerned with another social experiment, much less vicious, but one whose effects are less easily calculated and less easy to control. The conferring of an Anti-Social Behaviour Order, intended as a mark of disgrace and dishonour, has been regarded by some recipients as the opposite. The necessarily local scale within which the order has currency changes its value according to the premium placed on celebrity – especially in the form of notoriety – among those to whom other forms of distinction are unavailable. In this respect, there is almost a quaintness adhering to the criminal mug-shot displayed on Landy's medal, when compared to the inscrutability of the acronyms on the target-like disc of 'Virtual World' by Langlands and Bell. The ASBO has meaning only within the context of a 'knowable community', and is almost nineteenth century in conception, whereas the criminality associated with some of the organisations behind the acronyms in 'Virtual World' can only be assessed within a global context, within which different ideological perspectives would map the world according to diverse criteria of merit and demerit. Warfare in postmodernity is orientated increasingly towards ideological conflict rather than competition for territory, which makes the worldwide web, whose scope reverberates through the domain names on the reverse of the medal, a significant battleground in the war of definitions that has turned the history of medals into an extension of war by other means. Meanwhile, Felicity Powell's medal 'Hot Air', is a satirical reminder of the most significant form of territorial defeat in a war in which there are only losers. Global warming is the product of an excessively technologised biosphere, but the two sides of Powell's medal are equally unswerving in their denunciation of the source of the problem: in the human condition for which technology is only an aggrandised form of prosthesis; and in the arrogance of a species whose self-indulgence has often been in direct proportion to its talent for self-deception.

The liveliest episodes in the history of satirical medals have almost always involved visual expressions of the right to free speech, or of resistance to censorship, or have trained their focus on banned or taboo subject matter. Among those artists featured in the current exhibition, those who have lived for long periods of their lives under oppressive regimes exemplify the extremes of direct and indirect forms of challenge to authority. The savage humour of William Kentridge's assault on complicity in political injustice almost leaps out of the chosen medium, literally projecting from the surface of the medal, while the coded reticence of the Kabakovs' subversions is folded calmly into its structural ambiguities. The unmanageable centre of attention in Kentridge's saw-toothed vision of social and political abuse is an autonomous megaphone, a classic emblem of the means of amplifying one point of view in order to drown out others; the megaphone is the instrument of political oratory, of spokesmanship, the essential prosthesis for those who wish to speak for the people rather than allow them to speak for themselves. In Kentridge's vision, it has been disconnected, uprooted and given a roving commission, no longer transmitting the voice of a human agent, since the conceptual wiring that would sustain the illusion of sincerity has long since decayed, its fundamental message a repetitive confirmation to the listeners that they are screwed.

Perhaps the most enigmatic and most powerfully elliptical of the medals on display is that of Ilya and Emilia Kabakov. Their exclusive focus on the image of a single fly, resembling the presentation of a zoological specimen that stands in for an entire species, is also one instance of a thematic preoccupation that they have returned to several times in their work. Each return to this imagery reinforces the terms of a fictional theory that associates the collective behaviour of flies with the social politics of the totalitarian state. That the single fly can be regarded as a synecdoche for this complex of associations is confirmed by the drawing shown as part of the installation, 'The Life of Flies', where the anatomical drawing in black is enclosed within a diagram outlined in red representing the sum total of flies in the atmosphere above the Soviet Union. The symmetrical shape of this gigantic swarm indicates the highly organised principles that govern the lives of these insects, whose 'civilisation' generates patterns that reveal its symbiosis with the fortunes of the Soviet state. It is usually the bee, with its industriousness and cooperativeness, that is chosen as the fabled exemplar of civic responsibility in a well-run community, rather than the fly, with its associations of opportunism, parasitism, abjection and decay. The disjunction between the utopian programming of the communist era and the historical reality of mismanagement and waste is both explained away and mystified by the controlling agency of the fly, whose impact on human society is well in excess of Biblical proportions, since according to the Kabakov's satirical theory, the upper limit of the swarm is 60,000 kilometres above the earth. The medal of dishonour identifies the fly as culprit in the assessment of 'turning-points in our history that are still unexplained from the point of view of human behaviour'(The Life of Flies), an identification whose absurdity is bound to prompt reflection on the role of human agents whose behaviour has resembled that of flies, not in respect of the abstract beauty of their orchestrated movements, but in their scavenging for the rich pickings to be gleaned from a dying carcase. The apparent neutrality of the image belies its conceptual subtext, and provides a telling example of the unique properties of the medal in its ability to compress and encode a host of contingent details, telescoping an astonishing array of polemical issues in its presentation of a world in little.

What this exhibition also provides is a microcosm of the world of art, in its drawing together the designs of painters, cartoonists, sculptors, installation artists and filmmakers. There can be no other medium in which the limitations placed on size, shape, volume and colour have been so consistent throughout the history of its use. It is the great paradox of the discipline imposed by those limitations that it should have liberated so many artists of radically different traditions, practices and outlooks to be so outspoken in their engagement with issues of general public concern and with a sense of historical urgency, and all within the compass of something that can be held in the palm of the hand. The division of the history of medals into the parallel traditions of rewarding honour and berating dishonour has maintained the tension between dignified restraint and iconoclastic verve that has guaranteed the vitality of a medal-making culture that shows no signs of abating.

2009

Asymmetries in the Bush

There are two paintings in the Art Gallery of Western Australia – one from settler culture, the other aboriginal – that capture something of the significance of walking in the different conceptual worlds that co-exist in Australia. The one that translates very easily into European forms of experience is Frederick McCubbin's 1889 painting 'Down on his luck', which shows a single bushman, physically and psychologically isolated in the landscape. The human figure is relegated to one side of the canvas, allowing the wilderness to take centre stage. The bushman's pose, with head resting on one hand, recalls the classic European emblems of melancholy. Like the figure in Durer's 'Melencolia', he is very clearly abstracted from his environment, brooding on past and future rather than on present circumstance. His connection with the landscape seems minimal, and his campfire provides a diversion from it. The bush in this painting is simply a tract of land that has to be got through, that separates starting point and destination, hopes and disappointments, fears and desires whose setting and performance is always elsewhere. It is a medium for obstruction and delay, a catalyst for introspection, an objective correlative for 'bad luck', a scenography of absence. It is a landscape that does not communicate.

The other painting is a typical example of Nyoongar art in which footprints dominate in representations of the walkabout tradition that reasserts the continuity of the indigenous relationship to the land. This continuity is the most long-standing in cultural history, and its expression is the most deep-rooted in the history of art, with conventions that relate directly to the iconography of the rock art of the Dampier Archipelago, dating back thirty thousand years. The particular painting I have in mind is a contemporary work that includes icons of 13 human figures, 91 trees and 173 footprints.[16] The preponderance of footprints is appropriate to a culture in which everyone moved backwards and forwards between the coast and the highland scarp of what is now known as the Darling Range, occupying a variety of different sites according to the seasons of the year. There were six seasons:

---

16 I have made this painting sound anonymous, but it wasn't. In the time between assembling my notes and writing this account, one of my notebook pages went astray, the very one that recorded the artist and title of the work in question. Several attempts to retrieve the missing information – attempts made by Kate Fagan and others as well as by me – have proved unsuccessful, which means that I must take the unwanted responsibility for appearing not to take seriously the Aboriginal artistry that has been sidelined for much of Australian cultural history. My intention was to place it centre stage, but perhaps there is something inevitable about this parapraxis, about this slippage in a revisionist account that has not quite acknowledged its proximity to the intellectual habits of a colonial culture, habits that I might have assumed I could undo at will.

Birak (December and January) – summer, hot and dry
Bunuru (February and March) – early autumn
Djeran (April and May) – late autumn, cooler
Makuru (June and July) – early winter, cold and wet
Djilba (August and September) – late winter / early spring,
    warmer
Kambarang (October and November) – late spring, decreasing
    rain

Moves would be dictated by the availability of different foodstuffs in given places at specific times of year. Further moves would be required for attendance at ceremonial gatherings. To Western eyes, the picture plane resembles a kind of map, and in many artworks by the Nyoongar, footprints are arranged in series to indicate customary tracks. These tracks are more than convenient, they are definitive of the people's relationship with the land and with the Waugals (the water snake spirits) that created it. Even when attempts were made to erase these ancestral trails, the Nyoongars always remembered where they were. After 1829, when the port city of Fremantle was established, many Nyoongar tracks were bisected by settlers' walls and fences. The Nyoongar ignored these, even walking through houses from the back door to the front in order to follow traditional routes.

There is pathos in both representations: in the experience of the itinerant worker whose contact with the bush only deepens the alienation that has been transplanted to Australia along with European living and working conditions; and in the experience of an indigenous people dispossessed of its sacred sites but renewing in its art (as in its song) its claim to identification with the land. Both involve a measure of projection, and an elision of 'bad' history, which in the settler tradition is dealt with through marginalisation, by imposing a condition of mobility on those who do not qualify for civic status. The bushman belongs in Australian settler mythology, but does not belong in any local community. That exclusion is camouflaged through romanticisation, especially in the works of the Heidelberg school, of which McCubbin was a member, although none of these works escapes the ambivalence that is close to the surface in 'Down on his luck'. In the Nyoongar canvas, the details of settler life do not figure at all, as if they existed in another dimension, a false reality, a gaudy backcloth that the indigenous artist folds up and puts away.

It is, of course, impossible to walk though the bush as if stepping into the world of McCubbin or of Nyoongar art. Yet people do walk; they walk thousands of kilometres along carefully prepared trails such as the Bibbulmun Track, which stretches from the outskirts of Perth down to the south coast at Albany. The motivation to walk is partly to hunt, not for anything in fur or feathers, but for a ghost, the merest notion even, of an authenticity we are reluctant to let slip, to vanish altogether before we have gone to the trouble of looking for it. Part of the difficulty is knowing where to look. The Bibbulmun Track itself is a false reality, although it crosses places where the Bibbulmun people deepened their imprint on the landscape through habits acquired over thousands of years; it was marked out for the first time in 1974 by employees of the Forests Department, but had to be revised almost constantly in the face of pressure over bauxite mining, commercial forestry and water catchment issues. The track is a post-industrial construct, patched together from what was available, and it came into being the moment that walking became recreational, when the simplest activity that characterises the human made more sense in a culture of leisure than in a culture of necessity. The paradox of free time is the imperative it brings to explore space; not the space of our daily lives, but any space that lies beyond our daily habitus, for beyond is where authenticity seems to dwell, down pathways we need to follow to escape the staleness of modern life. The danger this brings is of over-investment in luxury, in what enriches our time too easily, so that we lose all respect for the value of what impoverishes us; rather than finding ways to slow that impoverishment down, and planning to make it stop. The modern desire to walk is really to stand still, to make the self a gauge for the frequencies and time-scales of all those orders of being we are out of touch with; but as things are, being in touch with these different orders is to be out of our own measure, and the only real choice we can make is to hesitate, between frequencies, between measures, between acceptance and denial.

It is hard enough to do this in the landscape of our up-bringing, the very setting of our orientation in the world, of the way we learned to take our bearings in it unreflect-ingly. But to hesitate over the way we fit into a strange landscape, as if choosing between different frames, or dif-ferent sets of pictorial conventions, is close to impossible, given the strong compulsion we are under to translate the strange into familiar terms, an act of translation we per-form before reflecting on it. For the present writer, the memory of walking ancient tracks in Britain is the default position, the almost mechanically applied template for orientation in, interpretation of, and cultural projection onto, other landscapes. Their ancientness is both authentic and inauthentic, even in the case of the oldest paths across the southern uplands, since their precise route is subject to change, and has changed often within living memory, although their proximity to the chalk ridges guarantees proximity to ancient settlements and field systems, to the funerary monuments of the Neolithic and the Bronze Age, and to Iron Age hill forts. Walking in chalk downland, over bare turf with scatterings of flint, is a rare encounter with emptiness and space in an overcrowded island, although it is simultaneously an immersion in human prehistory; Britain often seems like an island inundated by stories told and untold, and our ignorance of many of them is a reminder of those languages once used to evoke the landscape but now beyond reach. The lavishness with which the land has been described over the last two thousand years is in part a compensation for this loss.

Equipped with the cultural phenomenology of the British walker and enough food for four days (sliced cheese, dried fruit, peanuts, pitta bread, tea, powdered soup and rice) I started out on the Bibbulmun one day in early spring. The precise route had been mapped for me by the western Australian poet Glen Phillips. Glen had primed me, liberally and humorously, for a few days in Perth, and then sent me off to Bunbury, where a friend and spirit-guide had been persuaded to drive me into the hills.

The local psychopomp dropped me by the side of the Harvey-Quindanning Road, just north of the Murray River, with only three hours to go before dark. The track wound up through scrub and then forest. According to the map, the elevation rose from six hundred to nine hundred feet within the first kilometre. There were twelve kilometres to cover before reaching the Dookanelly campsite. I did not relish spending my first night by the side of the track, and reluctantly started to jog. I had made my pack as light as possible but it did not feel like it.

By the time I arrived at Dookanelly I was in a muck sweat. Stress and irritation must have been written all over me as I trudged out of the dark and into the glow of the campfire, but if the two fire-tenders, Roy and Janet, recognised this, they did not show it. I found a spot to unroll my sleeping bag, decanted some water from the rainwater butt, and paid a visit to the earth closet. An enormous Huntsman spider, as big as a toilet lid, was spanning the entrance to Avernus. I decided not to disturb it and paid my visit further off where the night life was invisible and ignorance was bliss. Roy and Janet turned out to be from Hampshire. I had flown eleven thousand miles, caught the train from Perth, had bussed and begged lifts to get to the drop-off point, had marched like a Roman legionary into the blackest night I had ever seen, and was able to spend the evening talking about chalk streams that rose less than thirty miles from the place where I had grown up. Roy reminisced about tickling trout in the River Meon. My surname, Mengham, is taken from the name of a village on Hayling Island, a few miles east of the point where the Meon falls into the Solent. The map of that area is full of Men- and Meon- prefixes. I remembered sitting by the Meon at dusk one summer when the air was full of swallows catching the flies the trout were also jumping for. This had been in the village of Meonstoke, where the Saxon church contained eleventh-century mural paintings commemorating St Swithin's conversion of the Meonwaras, the last British tribe to succumb to Christianity. Earlier in the year I had found the long barrow which had been the collective burial place of their Neolithic predecessors. It was further up the same valley. I had looked for it on an earlier occasion, but that had been in June when the grass was at its highest. Although the earthwork was marked on the map there was nothing to be seen. When I came back in December, an hour before sunset, the shadows began slowly to fill the slightest impressions in the turf, as if the landscape was remembering everything that had happened to it, and as I watched, the long barrow limned itself, the dark outline swelling. The long bar of light came to rest on the ground, and the true proportions of the monument were restored, as if it were projecting a dream of itself, of its lost volume, of its reserves of power, as a place in which the most important ideas of an entire culture once dwelled.

I had plenty of time to mull this over during the night, which was much colder than I was prepared for. I had no tent, only a sleeping bag. Most walkers I met during the next five days carried a roll of thin mattress material, but I had nothing to cushion my joints and spent most of each night aching and restless. I realised I would not discover any physical features that could locate the past for me, despite the depth of time the landscape had been inhabited. The Nyoongars had not led a settled existence before the arrival of the Dutch and the English, so there would be no evidence of permanent structures. But neither would there be any material remains of a nomadic culture. A European archaeologist would bank on finding tool-making debris or butchered animal bones to establish the presence of Mesolithic hunter-gatherers, but on the Bibbulmun these would remain as invisible as the Nyoongars' traditional paths, obliterated by countless cycles of burn-back and forest regrowth. The Aboriginal connection with the land could now only be traced through the incidence of certain plants and animals. Most of these remained unknown to me, or if I saw them I did not recognise them. But mostly I did not see them, and I seldom regretted this. I kept noticing holes in the banks to right and left of the path, where I knew the poisonous dugite snake must live, only two feet away from my legs. My vigilance was wonderful, but it was not rewarded until the third day, when I watched the last six inches of a dugite – pale underbelly, dark back – disappear into an old log.

I walked slowly, with long pauses to look and listen, and was irked not to encounter any decent-sized animals. The trail ran more or less parallel to the Murray, often quite close to the river, which must have been the main water supply for anything with a serious metabolism. On the higher slopes, there were many signs of where the wild pigs had been rooting, and on one occasion I made certain of identifying an emu print. It did not comfort me to read that emu parenting was conducted by aggressive males, or that in 1932 Western Australian farmers had had to use Lewis machine guns to stop a series of emu attacks.[17]

The only company I had during the second day was that of birds, and clouds of mosquitoes drifting by in the sunlight. There was a small, grey-coloured, long-tailed bird with a relaxed, see-sawing call that I thought was a white-breasted robin. I was amazed by the hovering flight pattern that sent it backwards and forwards over the same short distance as if entangled in a net. Often the birds were as inquisitive about me as I was about them, especially the large, white sulfur-crested cockatoos, swooping in relays from tree to tree, keen to escort me off the premises. The flora was easier to identify, but not that easy; except in the case of ferns, the only plants that looked exactly the same as in the northern hemisphere, and the ubiquitous balga, or grass tree, which had a profusion of uses for indigenous people. Its flowering grass-like stems produced edible gum and could be used for lighting fires. The leaves were used as

---

17 If I had known better, I would not have taken the guide book at face value, and would have been less jittery. As John Kinsella has pointed out, to represent the emu as vicious is a travesty. The drought conditions of 1932 meant that large numbers of emus were searching for water in farm land that they would normally keep away from. Anxious farmers jumped the gun – literally – and called in the army. Their excessive use of fire-power was condemned at the time as absurd.

roofing and bedding. The trunk was a larder full of witchetty grubs, a good source of protein, and the resin served as a powerful cement for constructing tools. When a grass tree eventually dies, its top disappears, as if carried off like a trophy. The denuded, black, hollow trunks are everywhere, resembling vacated termite mounds.

After a full day's walking from Dookanelly, I forded one last stream before reaching the Murray campsite, using red laterite stones the exact same colour as the doleritic earth. Standing in mid-stream, I could hardly hear the river, lapping faintly around half-submerged trees but otherwise without a murmur. Suddenly I noticed an old bicycle bell nailed to a tree on the far bank. In its small way, a warning of the traffic to come, it made the only mechanical sound in eighty miles. It came to me that I had not looked up all day, there had been no passing aircraft, but here was a gap in the forest canopy, and something was moving into it: a small cloud, looking like the crab nebula, not very far above.

As night fell on the Murray campsite, a posse of red-tailed black cockatoos passed overhead. Every five minutes for the last half hour of daylight a different species had flown up river, but already my attention had been diverted towards three human specimens, carefully bedding down around separate campfires. There was Lara, who had completed the day's walk two hours before the others, waiting impatiently for the dark to come so she could go and swim naked in the river; there was Bob, a long musician with white hair and an English accent, who called across to me with reminiscences about drinking in Cambridge pubs; and there was Kim, whose small pebbly glasses, Edwardian pointed beard and hunched shoulders made him look like a Poirot of the outback. Like Poirot, Kim was always sifting evidence, but he did not look for it beyond the pile of thick hardback books he had pulled out of his backpack. It turned out he was slowly working his way through all of Gore Vidal's sagas of American history. His days were spent rushing between camps to get on to the next chapter, pounding through the bush with the aid of two walking poles. He spoke few words and inscribed even fewer (just his first name and surname in the visitors' book that Roy and Janet had embellished with a cartoon and the legend 'Leave me here. I want to die'). Kim's obsessive progress was fuelled by narratives of engrossment, annexation, take-over; of territory, stock, manpower, and investment opportunities. The American myth of expansion, extracting and exhausting natural resources, followed an arc from east to west and from a finite, physical reality to the plumbless reservoir of the imagination, where it just kept going, further and deeper, and faster than anywhere else. It seemed absurd to correlate Vidal's fantasies of authentic imperialism with a walk in the bush, but the conversion of leisure time into an allegory of work, with the quickening of pace qualifying as productivity, enterprise, capital accumulation, had transformed Kim's walking tour into a parody of the game with high stakes in which he had never been able to compete. He barged about among the trees, unstable embodiment of a force that impels walkers of the city streets, caught up in a rhythm of mechanical indifference to the detaining pleasures of slow time, the stirrings of obscure creatures, the dehiscing undergrowth. But the text he continued to read, or write, in his head all day was no less fictitious than the maps used by all those passing through the narrow green corridors of the Bibbulmun, which was after all the dream of a bureaucrat with itchy feet, forest wallpaper lining a passageway in the conservation department, virtual heritage. The vast majority of names given to rivers, peaks, gorges and other natural features, not to mention roads, farms, mines and settlements, were either English or taken from other European languages.

The path leading north from the Murray campsite was scarred by the violent puncture marks of Kim's walking poles, many filled with rainwater that had collected in the night. After only fifteen minutes' walk, all my clothes were soaked through, since many of the forest leaves were designed to trap as much moisture as possible. The ferns were uncurling vigorously after a good drink, while the tree ferns resembled a display of inverted shower heads. The many spiders' webs, beaded with miniature droplets, were especially dense where the path joined forces with a creek. The junction was marked by a hastily assembled rubble of doleritic rocks. Even the birdcalls were affected by the weather. One soloist in particular recalled the sound of an improvising washboard.

Around mid-day, I stepped on the remains of a fire in the middle of the trail, showing that not everyone reaches camp before nightfall. After that, the path climbed steadily to a thousand feet where it was crossed frequently by kangaroo trails – the Oz equivalent of sheep tracks in England – and then began the descent into a valley lined with black, shattered rocks and cool pine forests. The bird sounds fell away in this Mediterranean ambience, apart from the gushing cries of two Splendid Fairy-Wrens preparing to forage. It was at this point I made the astounding discovery I could hear better with the hat-cord tucked behind my ears instead of in front of them...

The third night was spent at the Swamp Oak campsite, where I joined the two brothers Mark and Russell. Russell had damaged his shoulder badly and had been hoping to find a chiropractor in Dwellingup (the small logging town that I was due to reach the following day) but he had had no luck and was forced to choose between carrying on or abandoning the idea of walking the length of the trail. He had decided to press on, although he could only walk for twenty minutes before having to stop. The brothers were prone to bicker more often than not, and it struck me that Mark's best chance of tricking Russ into speeding ahead was to get him into a huff. Their mutual exasperation was beginning to reach a pitch when we were joined at the point of dusk by a party of four, somewhat delirious, middle aged women laden with baggage and supplies. Dolly, Nancy, Wendy ('Wen') and Cassie flopped down and proceeded to screech, hoot, cackle and whistle for the next three hours, which was the length of time it took them to cook spaghetti bolognese followed by cinnamon bun and custard. They freely admitted they were the only people who had actually put weight on while following the trail. I crept off to my sleeping bag at 9.30, already frozen, but soon fell into a heavy sleep that lasted half the night, despite the constant revelry.

The next day passed quickly. Notwithstanding my four hours of rest, I was now desperate for uninterrupted sleep, my thoughts were sometimes hard to focus and there was a curious effect of magnification on the edges of my vision. A swelling on my left knee was itching badly and I worried that the cause might be a kangaroo tick. I began to fixate on the Community Hotel I would reach by evening, on its restaurant, its bathrooms, and above all its beds. I thought of the pint of lager awaiting John Mills at the end of his desert trek in the film 'Ice Cold in Alex' and decided the equivalent for me would be 'Electric Blanket in Dwellingup'. The trail was strewn with shattered red rock, the whole area seemed to be breaking up in the wake of repeated forest fires. Nothing was intact apart from the great bare sheets of granite among pine trees that were lit by dazzling shafts of sunlight. Young tree ferns were coming up out of the earth like musical staves, while an unseen bird nearby was singing the two bar blues. There was another birdcall, perhaps that of a golden whistler, which took the form of a militaristic trill, a kind of brittle nineteenth-century march that I can still hear in my head. Not long before reaching Dwellingup I crossed some patches of private land that had been fiercely logged. Two entire hills had been blasted and now resembled an elephant's graveyard dotted with a few huge immoveable gum trees totally fire-blackened. On the forest fringe were two kookaburras, howling with glee.

The hotel had everything I needed: a communal shower, steak and chips, a whole bottle of red wine, and a king-sized electric blanket. After these miracles of solace and ease, the bush retreated into the imagination, back to the place it had come from, in the continent I had brought with me, the one in my head. I felt that I had walked to one side, or between, stretches of the real bush. The people I had met had all been white and urban, with no relationship to traditions of life in the forest. Nothing I had seen or heard spoke to me in its own language, I had given it subtitles in a faux documentary scripted in advance. The conventions of Aboriginal art now seemed anomalous, more eccentric, more archival than before, more lost.

I had not finished walking entirely; there was still one excursion to make from Dwellingup that passed by the Holyoake townsite. This had been settled in 1910 and abandoned in 1961. Everyone who ever lived there had been equal in the eyes of the South West Timber Hewers Cooperative Society. They had logged the immensely hard jarrah wood for railway sleepers that had been sold all over the world. But the market had tailed off and the mill closed in 1958. Holyoake was dying before it was wiped out in the Dwellingup bush fires of 1961. The place was over and done with but had the air of unfinished business. The buildings had been levelled down to the height of a single brick. The fabric had deteriorated much more seriously than my own body during the same time. I wandered through the remains of mill, school and several cottages, and came to the edge of everything. Beyond were hundreds of miles of forest. It was good to think of three generations being raised in a spirit of equality, but their collective livelihood would have depended on the removal of the indigenous peoples. The Nyoongars would always return in the year following any bush fire, but modern commerce is a series of extinction events, and its cycles are the ghosts in the insurance machine. The forest is the risk assessor's Sublime. With the townsite just behind me, and the hat-cord behind my ears, I was picking up star-noise, insect frequencies, marsupial wave bands; but in the void beyond that there was the silence of dead languages, of entire language families, organised around the words for all those attitudes and activities I had not performed in the bush. I could not have been further from the landscape of southern England, but I could not have been closer to its passage in time between history and prehistory. There was no need to take a step further in Australia, and no point, since all I had done, or could do, was to walk in the bubble of my own language, with its shrink-wrapped baggage allowance, and its cultural carry-on.

2009

Strange Weather

I want to try to account for the allure of Giorgione's painting known as 'La Tempesta'. This work has mystified art historians of the Renaissance, but it has also seduced art-lovers with no special knowledge of Renaissance ico-nography. When I say 'mystified', I mean that it has di-vided art historians, many of whom have been convinced by their own interpretations while remaining sceptical of others. Edgar Wind believed that the choice of figures – that of a soldier and a young woman with an infant – was a standard Renaissance pairing designed to recommend the combining of *fortezza* with *carita*.[18] Maurizio Calvesi has since argued that the female figure represents the earth it-self, pointing to the extent of early sixteenth-century fas-cination with the idea of a *copula mundi*, an act of union between the feminine earth and a masculine '*elemento fecon-datore*' identified with '*il moto celeste virile*'.[19] And Jaynie An-derson has offered a detailed reading of the painting, con-necting it with a scene from Francesco Colonna's romance *Hypnerotomachia Poliphili*, in which the young hero Poliphilo encounters the goddess Venus in his quest for the spirit of antiquity. Anderson records a number of parallels in the imagery of both painting and romance, including 'broken columns, the miraculous appearance of Venus suckling Cupid, and the fantastic architecture'; and she finds irre-sistible the possibility that the prominence of the column alludes to Colonna's own surname.[20] The problem with all these attempts to explain the symbolism of the painting is that they depend on a guarantee that what Giorgione means to represent with his pair of figures is an attempt,

18 Edgar Wind, Giorgione's 'Tempesta': with comments on Giorgione's poetic allegories (Oxford, 1969), p.3.

19 Maurizio Calvesi, 'La Tempesta di Giorgione', in Giorgione e la cultura Veneta tra '400 e '500: mito, allegoria, analisi iconologica (Roma: De Lucca, 1981), p.54.

20 Jaynie Anderson, Giorgione: the painter of poetic brevity (Paris: Flammarion, 1997), p.168.

or a desire, or the necessity, to unite them. Even a casual observation of the painting suggests something very different; the two figures are about four metres apart, they are physically separate and mentally isolated. They do not propose the inevitability of embrace, or of recognition, or of any reciprocity at all. They appear divergent rather than convergent and their juxtaposition does not make them stand out from the rest of the painting but enables them to frame and support a landscape infused with a mood of uncertainty, vulnerability, suspense, and even of menace. The change of names given to the canvas (we do not know what title Giorgione himself had in mind) from 'The Soldier and the Gypsy' to 'The Tempest' reflects a growing awareness on the part of viewers that the real focus of the work might not be the *dramatis personae* but the overall atmosphere of the scene in which they are placed. If Giorgione is trying to call to mind the potential cooperation of *fortezza* and *carita*, the counterpointing of the earth and celestial motion, or the gravitation of Poliphilo towards the figure of Venus, his point is surely that the conjunction hinted at in each of these scenarios is precisely what is being suspended; what is being kept quite literally beyond arm's length.

Pietro Zampetti goes as far as to claim that the landscape plays a part equal to that of the human figures in generating a pervasive mood or, one might almost say in the style of Auden, a distinctive climate of opinion: '[the paintings of Giorgione] *mostrano che il paesaggio assume per l'artista altrettanto importanza, come espressione di stato d'animo, quanto le figure*'.[21] However, Zampetti associates this condition with a timeless truth rather than with a time-bound reality: '*L'arte di*

---

21 Pietro Zampetti, 'La quiete dopo La Tempesta', in *Giorgione e l'umanesimo Veneziano*, ed. Rodolfo Pallucchini (Firenze: Olschki, 1981), p.292.

Giorgione e essenzialmente contemplativa, non si lega al contingente, quando all'assoluto.[22] But if the historical analysis of the leading motifs seems unsatisfying, this does not necessarily lead to an ahistorical contemplation of the background; rather, it arouses curiosity about the historical origin of the state of mind projected into every aspect of the painting, the psychology distilled into the strange weather still enchanting viewers many centuries after the moment of composition.

That moment came at some point in the years between 1505 and 1510 (I have stretched the period in question to allow for a range of conjectures about the chronology; a majority of commentators are in favour of the much narrower interval 1506–08). At the beginning of the sixteenth century, storms depicted in works of art were commonly identified with *Fortuna* in her aspect of bad luck; but if we look beyond the iconography to the weather reports of the period and to the adverse fortunes of the Venetian Republic at home and abroad, we find a remarkable coincidence of natural disasters, industrial accidents and military stand-offs. There were earthquakes in Crete (controlled by the Republic), killer storms in the Adriatic, conflagrations around the Rialto and, towards the end of this period, an explosion at the Arsenale so massive it covered the entire city with a thick cloud of dark smoke: '*habitaque pro ostento res fuit*' notes Pietro Bembo in the Latin text of his *Historia Veneta* ['the incident was taken as a portent'].[23] But by far the most sinister influence on the prevailing mood of the Venetians during this period was the threat of a German invasion. Maximilian actually did invade the Tyrol and Friuli, prompting the Senate to levy soldiers throughout the mainland territories, and in the period 1507–08, precisely

22 Ibid, pp.291–2.
23 Pietro Bembo, *Historia Veneta* (1551), Liber Septimus, p.62.

the interval to which the execution of the painting has been most frequently assigned, there was a series of nasty engagements between the two armies.

The male figure in Giorgione's composition is a soldier contemplating a vulnerable young woman and child; the deadlocked meanings of the painting are not unconnected to the prolonged military stalemate in the Veneto that was underway for a significant part of this time, and the historical limbo in which the Venetians existed for a number of years is reflected in the mutual wariness of the two figures, in the tense waiting game that holds them in relation. Any Venetian would have connected the portrayal of a soldier with the problem of the Germans during this period, but Giorgione could not have kept the connection out of his mind; he would have been supersensitive to its implications, since he was in the process of painting frescoes in the newly rebuilt *Fondaco de' Tedeschi*, the trading centre for German merchants that had burned down in 1505, in one of Fortuna's many strokes of bad luck during the first decade of the sixteenth century. The woman in Giorgione's painting cannot be said to welcome the presence of the soldier, her attitude is a guarded one. If I hesitate to put it more strongly than that, it is because any more would detract from the powerful reticence that is widely recognised as the condition for inclusion in Giorgione's imaginative world. But we cannot pretend that the Venetians would have hesitated for a moment to anticipate the causes of apprehension, or the nature of the threat posed by the figure of a soldier in the Veneto at this time. During the siege of Cormons in 1508, the Venetian commander Giorgio Corner was under no illusion about the need to protect the female population from violation by the troops by locking them inside a church: '*Cornelius mulieres omnes, uno in templo compulsas, ab iniuria militum defendit'.*[24]

We could say of 'The Tempest' that it is partly the study of a passage in time, of a time when the future was uncertain; but it is also a very Venetian painting in its attention to the insubstantiality of place, to the geographical presence of a state whose physical foundation has been conjured up out of nothing. There is a bridge at the very centre of the painting; like Venice itself, Giorgione's landscape is an extended bridge passage, a long-drawn out moment of transition, exhibiting an awareness of being suspended between two pieces of *terra firma*, and between two sets of stable conditions: between night and day, between town and country, between nature and culture. But most of all, it is about being stranded, exposed, vulnerable, lost between the ruins of the past and a future struggling to be born, with small chance of survival, to a single mother overlooked by a male witness who might conceivably be on the look-out in the guise of protector, or who might be closing in on the last woman trying to escape the infanticide of a sixteenth-century Herod. In which case, this is an updated Bethlehem in an alternative universe, in the history of a Christianity that never happened, of a Venice in peril, of a city that defined itself as the bridge between East and West, as the barrier between Christian and Muslim worlds. And its entire ideological reason for being is crumbling at a touch, collapsing into a black hole. Giorgione's 'La Tempesta' was created in the same *episteme* as Antonella da Messina's *Annunciation*, that astonishing painting in which the Virgin is shown in the middle of a deep distraction, imagining all that might have been – the last reverie about a life gone forever – with her extended hand both warding off the angel and beginning to let go of everything the angel

24 Ibid, VII, p.32.

has banished, alternative histories of the world pivoting around a single moment.

2010

The Folding Telescope and Many Other Virtues of Bruno Schulz

Bruno Schulz was born and was killed in the Polish town of Drohobycz, now in the Ukraine. The road there from Lviv (which Schulz knew as Lwów) is today lined with barren fields. There are patches of cultivation a few yards off from the garden walls of roadside villas, but everywhere else the land is ragged with tares and other weeds. The long battle lines of combine harvesters tackling endless miles of grain can be watched only in old film stock, most of it black and white, or only in memory. The towns and villages have shed the more obvious emblems of Soviet uniformity, especially in Drohobycz itself, where an unusual number of old houses survives. Much of the town centre still looks like the environment that Schulz grew up in. In fact, the material remains of the command economy are more obsolescent than the physical evidence of a largely nineteenth-century townscape. On the outskirts are shunting yards full of rotting iron, with a classic Soviet billboard showing a cartoon Stakhanovite worker balancing a huge girder on one shoulder. These give way to acres of unused bricks, stacked mysteriously in a series of upside-down arches. The traffic slows when the hoarded debris of overproduction has been passed and you reach the edge of what feels like an older, more domestic economy. There is an apple orchard, with a black and red woodpecker resting on a telegraph pole. Across the street is a wooden house sporting bright new tin drainpipes. The clapboarding is cracked and warped, but this one storey dwelling sports a row of stylised metopes. Sparrows are having a dustbath on the pitted pavement outside. Next door, a small girl pushes a pink-clad Barbie doll through the ironwork of her front gate. A cockerel is crowing in the front yard. There is a garden area with a large and robust crop of dandelions and a shabby old hexagonal summer house, a compost heap propped against one side. Between the road and the pavement is a narrow verge with untidy stacks of hay at regular intervals. Schulz's own house is found at 10, Florianska Street. I approached it with two friends, poet Leo Mellor and translator Piotr Szymor. We stood under the walnut tree across the road to avoid a shower of rain.

It is a modest-sized house, one storey high and no more than 30ft by 12ft in area. During his adult years, Schulz was living in this space with four dependants. The style of the facade is neoclassical, with a certain amount of restrained plaster ornamentation and a disciplined repetition of elements. The arrangement of the five windows, however, with three on one side of the door and two on the other, introduces a curious asymmetry, which must have appealed to a writer whose imagination was quickened by opportunities to discompose the orderly and introduce subtle mutations into conventional appearances. It is impossible to see inside this dwelling for the simple reason that it remains, as it always was, a private residence, but there is something fitting, and even obscurely satisfying, in this gate-keeping, in this show of indifference to the literary pilgrim. Mere observation never reveals anything in Schulz's stories, where the substance of reality eludes every attempt to imprison it in the dead forms of everyday appearance. Schulz's entire universe is premised on the vitality of hidden life and encrypted purpose:

Everything diffuses beyond its borders, remains in a given shape only momentarily, leaving this shape behind at the first opportunity. A principle of sorts appears in the habits, the modes of existence of this reality: universal masquerade.[25]

The evidence of this organising principle is provoked by attempts to control the space, or spaces, within which it operates. The focal point for the reader's imagination as it is guided through Schulz's prose is movement through space; and this space is contested, drawn backwards and forwards imaginatively into different zones of power, different spheres of influence. Movement through space is subject to the influence of certain agencies, figures of authority whose status is according to profession, or seniority, or rank. The traction they exert on free movement triggers a process of masquerade, which often turns inside out the conventional distribution of power and powerlessness.

In the stories of Bruno Schulz, this principle of inversion is readily apparent in the relations between masters and servants. The servant class does not underpin the order presided over by its employers, but usurps the leading role. The most powerful figure in *Cinnamon Shops* is the servant girl, Adela. Similarly, the most childish of all the characters is the head of the household, Jacob. Schulz's world is one of systematic reversals, in which those in positions of social superiority experience the greatest degree of debasement, and *vice versa*. The dominant principle of duality in his books is established by metamorphosis, as evidenced in the following passage from the story, 'Cockroaches':

---

25 'Essay for Witkacy', in *Letters and Drawings of Bruno Schulz*, ed. Jerzy Ficowski (New York: Fromm, 1990), p.113.

In that rarely visited, festive room exemplary order had reigned since father's death, maintained by Adela with the help of wax and polish. The chairs all had antimacassars; all the objects had submitted to the iron discipline which Adela exercised over them. Only a sheaf of peacock's feathers standing in a vase on a chest of drawers did not submit to regimentation. These feathers were a dangerous, frivolous element, hiding rebelliousness, like a class of naughty schoolgirls who are quiet and composed in appearance but full of mischief when no longer watched. The eyes of these feathers never stopped staring; they made holes in the walls, winking, fluttering their eyelashes, smiling to one another, giggling and full of mirth. They filled the room with whispers and chatter; they scattered like butterflies around the many-armed lamps; like a motley crowd they pushed against the matted, elderly mirrors, unused to such bustle and gaiety; they peeped through the key-holes.[26]

The order so comprehensively disturbed here is associated with a military style of control – with an 'iron discipline'. It is undermined playfully at first by feathers compared to schoolgirls, but the relentless process of transformation that generates all of Schulz's prose soon intensifies this mischievousness into something more insistent and invasive, a more serious form of rebelliousness. The motif of the peacock's feather epitomises the Ovidian precedents for metamorphosis: the eyes on the tail were originally the eyes of *Argos panoptes*, the guardian – 'all eyes' – supposed to protect Io from rape by Zeus, a figure whose failed panopticism is reflected in the merely decorative eyes of the peacock's plumage. Schulz soon transmogrifies this inert

---

26 Bruno Schulz, The Complete Fiction (New York: Walker and Company, 1989), p.74.

association into a series of predicates of 'staring', 'winking', 'peeping'. The surveillance we might associate with military authority is gradually displaced and repudiated by the inquisitiveness of the unruly crowd in the street, and this systematic introduction of the carnivalesque is absolutely typical of Schulz, keeping in tension the opposing principles already included in the second clause of this passage, with a nearly oxymoronic invocation of the 'festive' room in which 'exemplary order' 'reigns' for the time being only.

Schulz's writing takes place more often than not in a series of unpredictable rooms, unpredictable especially when the rooms in question are usually avoided, ignored, even sealed off. It is precisely the most abandoned chambers that ferment hidden and uncontrollable forms of life. Niches, cubby-holes, attics, basements, cupboards, mouse-holes, forgotten rooms, are breeding grounds for the creatures of imagination that have been denied an existence in the rationalised space of everyday life. This supplementary form of life takes shape as an alternative, parallel universe whose interconnections with the familiar world become increasingly frequent and progressively overwhelming. Whole species of make-believe creatures begin to crowd into the already overpopulated suite of rooms where the narrator's family conducts its affairs. Both space and time are required to flex and bend in order to accommodate this prodigious multiplication of objects and characters. The fabric of the house is being constantly reorganised while the hours of the day and night become stretched and attenuated in the effort to engross the inordinate expansion of newly discovered contingencies.

Schulz's narrator recognises the need for desire to find new and additional sequences of time to do justice to its sheer plenitude. The story 'The Night of the Great Season' begins in precisely this vein:

Everyone knows that in a run of normal uneventful years that great eccentric, Time, begets sometimes other years, different, prodigal years which – like a sixth, smallest toe – grow a freak month...

There are people who liken these days to an apocrypha, put secretly between the chapters of the great book of the year; to palimpsests, covertly included between its pages; to those white, unprinted sheets on which eyes, replete with reading and the remembered shapes of words, can imagine colours and pictures, which gradually become paler and paler from the blankness of the pages, or can rest on their neutrality before continuing the quest for new adventures in new chapters.[27]

For Schulz, it is not only the excessiveness of individual desires that produces such a brilliant competition of realities, it is matter itself that is constantly reforming under the pressure of desire. Schulz's work is predicated on a fundamental lawlessness that is constantly threatening to disrupt the illusion of reality that the text is forever gravitating towards only to veer away from it at the last second. And yet the pretext for this illusion, or series of illusions, is evoked with an astonishing vividness. The environment of Schulz's fantastic characters and attendant beings is unignorably detailed, tangible, powerfully vital. Drohobycz and its surroundings are indelibly marked in the language that works so hectically to supplant them with day-dreams. Every inch of the town appears to teem with alternative story lines, while for Schulz it is also the materiality of language, in its capacity to generate new perceptions, new beings and entire spheres of existence that the text abandons itself to with such gusto and such energy.

---

27 Ibid, p.84.

In the street-scenes that are frequent in the illustrations to Schulz's stories, the buildings are commonly presented as a jumble of simple, box-like structures, whose modest scale in relation to the human figures makes them seem as impermanent and manipulable as an arrangement of toys.[28] They echo and enhance the protean imagination at the centre of the writing, with its proneness to reconfigure the architectural settings, both extending and abolishing space at will. Interior scenes, marked with an assortment of furnishings and impedimenta, are often presented as if taking place in an open area, such as a piazza or market place, with no walls between the background frieze of town houses and the foreground assemblage of figures, even when these are naked or *déshabillé*.[29] The figures tower over these spaces surrounded by pocket-sized houses, as if stranded in the centre of an architectural model, and yet the relations between background and foreground, between architecture and humanity, are further unsettled by giving dwarfish proportions to all the male characters. Joseph, the focal character in 'Sanatorium under the Sign of the Hourglass', is equipped with a tall funnel of a hat and a capacious overcoat that reaches almost to the ground. Its conspicuously large buttons help to give Joseph the appearance of a child dressing up in adult clothes, and whenever his figure is surrounded by those of other male characters, they are commonly bunched together in a way that recalls children ganging together in the open.[30] The townscape of the stories is seen with a kind of double vision that overlays the

28 See, for example, 'Joseph and Dr Gotard', *The Drawings of Bruno Schulz*, ed. Jerzy Ficowski (Evanstown: Northwestern University Press, 1990), p.191.

29 Ibid, p.230.

30 Ibid, p.227.

observations of a grown-up point of view with the memories of a child. But while the physical situation of the child is reflected in the frequency with which the objects of attention are seen from below, it is never the male adult characters that are elevated into positions of physical dominance, only women; women who are conspicuously inaccessible, statuesque, and contemptuous of the men around them. Female figures are always taller or, when reclining, longer than their male satellites in Schulz's illustrations. One particularly disturbing conflation of the child's point of view with that of the adult male submissive is the mural for a child's nursery commissioned by a Nazi officer who admired Schulz's work; in an adaptation of a Snow White scenario, this tableau depicts red-hatted-dwarves in the company of a tall, dark-haired female wearing a dress whose skirt reaches only to mid-thigh. The point of view is low enough for a child, but also low enough to reflect a desire to look under the skirt.

The gaze is baffled of course, since the desire is chiefly a desire to be rejected and degraded by the kind of tyrannical female found in a majority of Schulz's artworks. One of the most cherished images in Schulz's visual repertoire is that of Bianca, the aloof heroine of 'Spring'. Schulz never tired of producing variants on the scene in which Bianca is seen being driven in a carriage, her long legs extended and folded provocatively in a way that obscures the view of her father, seated passively beside her.[31] Her languorous, outstretched form contrasts with the hunched, precarious figure of the coachman in front of her, and his docility is magnified by the spectacle of tamed brute strength embodied in the powerful horses yoked to the carriage. In one striking version, the heads of both horses are twisted

31 Ibid, p.208.

round as if in homage to the imperious girl, and this conscription of domestic fauna in the general worship of dominant females is linked directly to male abjection.[32] Several of Schulz's drawings feature dogs cringing at the feet of one or more female figures, and in one variant illustration for 'Sanatorium', an elegantly dressed woman is seen walking between a representation of Schulz himself in subservient mode and a small dog.[33] This obvious counterpointing of inferior conditions is implied in all those drawings that include either men or animals overmastered by women.

There is an exhaustiveness in Schulz's pursuit of minute variations on the same theme that makes his visual work feel as if it is spiralling in on itself in an ever tightening knot of obsessions; by contrast, Schulz's writing is a process of uncoiling that retains the link to its axis, the hub of desire around which it turns, while it spools outwards, encircling new territories, inscribing new structures. Schulz himself recognised the difference in scope encompassed by his work in different media notwithstanding their common themes:

> If I am asked whether the same thread recurs in my drawings as in my prose, I would answer in the affirmative. The reality is the same; only the frames are different. Here material and technique operate as the criterion of selection. A drawing sets narrower limits by its material than prose does. That is why I feel I have expressed myself more fully in my writing.[34]

Despite the frequency of subjugation in the subject matter of Schulz's drawings and paintings, its constant

---

32 Ibid, p.209.
33 Ibid, p.233.
34 *Letters*, p.112.

reformulation does not share the paralyzing effect of commercial pornography, mainly because its various treatments do not simplify but complicate an underlying sexual compulsion by evoking other, historically specific, forms of social and cultural inequality. Perhaps the most troubling image of all is that of a stooping orthodox Jew who passes two women in evening wear; he is walking towards the viewer on an uneven path while they are ascending a short flight of steps in the opposite direction.[35] The Jew wears a broad-brimmed hat that casts a shadow over his face, accentuating his servile gaze towards the nearer of the two women who looks back and down with evident consciousness of her physical and social elevation, the whiteness of her skin and dress contrasting with the darkness of his face and clothes. Disdain for the Jew is commonly assumed to have an ethnic motivation, and there is little doubt that Schulz's perception of Polish habits of disparagement is tinged with an awareness of growing racial tensions during the Second Republic, but it has also absorbed the complexity of the Polish demographic in the early twentieth century. According to Norman Davies, Polish Jews belonged for the most part either to a 'small and wealthy bourgeoisie' or to a 'mass of urban artisans living by trades and crafts'.[36] Schulz, as a Jewish teacher of arts and crafts, occupied a sensitive position as a modestly paid professional whose discipline was closely related to the means of subsistence of many working class Jews. The stratification that characterised the relationship between class and ethnicity in a town like Drohobycz was one that Schulz performed in his everyday working practices.

35 *Drawings*, p.237.
36 Norman Davies, *Heart of Europe: A Short History of Poland* (Oxford: Clarendon press, 1984), p.120.

Masochism originated in the geographical vicinity of Drohobycz. Leopold von Sacher-Masoch was born in Lwow, in a building now occupied by the Hotel George. His father was the local Chief of Police, and the youthful Leopold was acutely aware of social, political, national and ethnic tensions in the area. His most famous narrative, *Venus in Furs* (1870), is set partly in Galicia, and includes several references to Lwów. One of the key phases in the degradation of its protagonist emphasises the importance of architectural as well as topographical contexts for its focus on the graduation of rank and on the ratio between physical restraint and imaginative freedom. The protagonist, Severin, is imprisoned in a cellar by his mistress Wanda, for an indefinite period of time that he himself is unable to measure. His release from this condition inaugurates a period of more intensive enslavement to Wanda – confinement underground serving as the prelude to sexual and social humiliation. The use of a cellar or basement as a corollary for psychological debasement recalls the specific pressure of desire on Schulz's fascination with hidden spaces, secret hiding places, unsuspected dimensions within domestic settings. Except that in Schulz's case, the order of priorities is almost reversed, with the psychology of debasement serving as a pretext or starting point for the exercise of the architectural imagination, for the multiplication and hierarchisation of imaginary spaces derived from a realistic original. The uncollected prose fiction 'The Republic of Dreams' consists of a series of variations on the theme of spatial ramification, worked out as a series of extrapolations on the townscape of Drohobycz:

> The garden plots at the outskirts of town are planted as if at the world's edge and look across their fences into the infinity of the anonymous plain. Just beyond the tollgates the

map of the region turns nameless and cosmic like Canaan. Above that thin forlorn snippet of land a sky deeper and broader than anywhere else, a sky like a vast gaping dome many stories high, full of unfinished frescoes and improvisations, swirling draperies and violent ascensions, opens up once again.[37]

It is as if the town encompasses the entire universe, its buildings reaching up into the sky to enclose infinity, while also establishing a system of gradations 'many stories high' that will allow for relative degrees of superiority and inferiority. In one of his letters to the poet Stefan Szuman, Schulz employs topographical and architectural metaphors to articulate the scope and limitations of the creative imagination:

> Those poems were a full and joyous experience for me; they were like an expansion of my own world into a new, strange, yet somehow familiar outlying region, the discovery in my town of some long-lost street. I may be wrong, but I feel we must have been on close neighbourly terms somewhere, as if we had once knocked against the same wall from opposite sides.[38]

Once again, Schulz celebrates the fertility of the imagination, its germinative power, in terms of architectural reproduction, while also tracing this process back to its origin in a single, self-enclosed space. It is a space that has overtones of confinement, and of an almost claustrophobic proximity, since it is under conditions of imprisonment

---

37 Published in *Tygodnik Ilustrowany*, no.29, 1936, and included in translation in *Letters*, pp.217–23.
38 Letter of 24 July, 1932, *Letters*, p.36.

that neighbours tend to communicate by knocking on walls. Schulz expresses with enthusiasm the extent to which his imaginative world is reflected in that of Szuman, while defining the exact degree of their reciprocity in terms of segregation. An almost passionate entertaining of the idea of affinity is contradicted by an architecture of aversion. There is an equivalent form of resistance in his attitude towards spending time with other people, conveyed in a letter to Tadeusz Brzeza: 'I can't stand people laying claim to my time. They make the scrap they touch nauseating to me. I am incapable of sharing time, of feeding on somebody's leftovers.'[39] The letter to Szuman seeks partly to flatter its recipient, while the letter to Brzeza does not broach the relationship between its writer and reader, but speaks in the abstract about fear of encroachment on the routines that structure Schulz's world. This fear is deep-seated enough to be described in terms of a physiological reaction. Schulz's fundamental response to the idea of sharing time and space with others on equal terms is one of allergic rejection, despite his many attempts to persuade others of his desire to make common imaginative cause with them. Earlier in the same letter to Brzeza, the relationship between architectural space and personal vulnerability is explored in a trope that makes the competition for time and space in the school where Schulz is employed a form of impingement that writes itself directly onto his body:

> For you must realise that my nerves have been stretched thin like a net over the entire handicraft centre, have crept along the floor, smothered the walls like tapestry and covered the [work]shops and the smithy with a dense web.

39 Letter of 2 December, 1934, Ibid, p.56.

This phenomenon is known to science as *telekinesis*, which makes everything that happens in the shops, the planing shed, and so on seem to happen directly on my skin as well.[40]

Schulz's nervous system is given the properties of a net, a web, and even a tapestry; and these different kinds of textile are identified with the text written directly on the skin. Nerves are meshed with language; writing embodies an acute sensitivity to pleasure and pain. Schulz understands his own writing as a means of working out a response to certain key images; he calls them images, but they are more like primal scenes, the imagination's version of childhood feelings that persist as adult anxieties and wishful thinking. They tend to amplify an acute vulnerability, a child's sense of being undefended, unprotected, even when they acknowledge the sincere efforts to reassure the child made by inadequate parental figures:

> Another of those images for me is that of a child carried by its father through the spaces of an overwhelming night, conducting a conversation with the darkness. The father caresses the child, folds him in his arms, shields him from the natural element that chatters on and on, but to the child these arms are transparent; the night cuts straight through them, and over the father's soothing words he hears its sinister blandishments without interruption.[41]

Schulz's attraction to eroticised forms of powerlessness must arise partly from the need to convert the impotence of these primal scenes into the basis of an adult resilience,

40 Ibid, p.55.
41 'Essay for S.I. Witkiewicz', *Letters*, p.110.

through the constant rehearsing of an equivalent dynamic. Schulz's own understanding of this process figures writing as a species of rewriting, an interminable practice of reconstituting the same elements, over and over again:

> These early images mark out to artists the boundaries of their creative powers. The works they create represent drafts on existing balances. They do not discover anything new after that, they only learn how to understand better and better the secret entrusted to them at the outset; their creative effort goes into an unending exegesis, a commentary on that one couplet of poetry assigned to them.[42]

The couplet is the poetic equivalent of the architectural confined space, and the exegesis conducted by Schulz's work across all media operates much more frequently through the registers of topography and architecture than through the register of poetry. The specific combination of subject matter and formal method in his writings and drawings can be thought of as manifesting a poetics of abasement. The endless variations on a primal scene that is never rendered conclusively simulates the building of a structure 'many stories high' over a basement that remains hidden. It is appropriate that Schulz's house on Florianska Street is only one storey high, and that the style chosen for that single storey would be better suited to a much larger building. Like so many nineteenth century dwellings across Poland and the Ukraine, the ambition to add further stories in subsequent stages of construction was never realised. The hoped-for prosperity that would allow this simply never materialised. In Schulz's case, the ambition was realised through a style of architectural exegesis

---

42 'Essay for S.I. Witkiewicz', *Letters*, p.111.

in writing. In text after text, the boundaries of a confined space were surpassed imaginatively through the exegetical expansion of space and time. Many of Schulz's scenes of writing resemble the confined space of a *camera obscura* entered by a panorama of the world outside. Perhaps the most tantalising exploration of this idea is found in 'Sanatorium Under the Sign of the Hourglass', in the episode where the chamber of the *camera obscura* itself is extended and articulated:

> The room behind the shop was still empty. Through a glass door some light filtered in from the shop. On the walls the shop assistants' overcoats hung from hooks. I opened the parcel and, by the faint light from the door, read the enclosed letter.
>
> The letter informed me that the book I had ordered was unfortunately out of stock. They would look out for it, although the result of the search was uncertain; meanwhile, they were sending me, without obligation, a certain object, which, they were sure, would interest me. There followed a complicated description of a folding telescope with great refractive power and many other virtues. Interested, I took the instrument out of the wrapping. It was made of black oilcloth or canvas and was folded into the shape of a flattened accordion. I have always had a weakness for telescopes. I began to unfold the pleats of the instrument. Stiffened with thin rods, it rose under my fingers until it almost filled the room; a kind of enormous bellows, a labyrinth of black chambers, a long complex of camera obscuras, one within another. It looked, too, like a long-bodied automobile made of patent leather, a theatrical prop, its lightweight paper and stiff canvas imitating the bulkiness of reality. I looked into the black funnel of the instrument and saw deep inside the vague outline of the back of the

Sanatorium. Intrigued, I put my head deeper into the rear chamber of the apparatus. I could now see in my field of vision the maid walking along the darkened corridor of the Sanatorium, carrying a tray. She turned round and smiled. 'Can she see me?' I asked myself. An overwhelming drowsiness misted my eyes. I was sitting, as it were, in the rear chamber of the telescope as if in the back seat of a limousine. A light touch on a lever and the apparatus began to rustle like a paper butterfly; I felt that it was moving and turning toward the door.

Like a large black caterpillar, the telescope crept into the lighted shop – an enormous paper arthropod with two imitation headlights on the front. The customers clustered together, retreating before this blind paper dragon; the shop assistants flung open the door to the street, and I rode slowly in my paper car amid rows of onlookers, who followed with scandalised eyes my truly outrageous exit.[43]

This curious apparatus, which undergoes a series of permutations from the moment it is unwrapped, has been sent to Joseph as a substitute for a book, which means that in some sense it must be understood as serving the same purpose as a book. Moreover, the book originally ordered by Joseph is supposed to be a pornographic text, which makes the characteristic stiffness and extensibility of the substitute machine correspond to the desired effect of pornographic stimulation. As the hand-held object grows in volume to such an extent that Joseph can climb inside it, it seems also to contain the entire geography of the story in which it features, allowing its protagonist to review once again the scene of his first arrival at the sanatorium.

43 'Sanatorium Under the Sign of the Hourglass', *Complete Fiction*, pp.254–6.

The moving 'complex of camera obscuras' epitomises the dynamic of Schulz's text, which circles obsessively and disproportionately around a single point of origin, its exegetical energy fuelled by desire, and its capacity for infinite transformation signaled by the conjunction of references to caterpillar and butterfly. And the narrator's pleasure at being considered outrageous is an index of Schulz's achievement in effecting the metamorphosis of powerlessness into pleasure, ensuring that compulsion is always given enough scope to expand into creativity.

2011

Essaying
The Habitus of the Text

The movement of thought in Montaigne's essays, composed and recomposed over a period of twenty years, is hesitant, impulsive, easily distracted, decoyed by sudden enthusiasms, snared by the memory of other texts, lured by the reflecting fragments of similar preoccupations in the minds of others. It is above all else a movement inward and outward, attentive to the occasions of thinking and writing, to the circumstances of time and place in which an 'attempt' is made (an 'essai') to compose something out of scattered materials, out of the books that chance to be at hand, the ideas that happen to rise to the surface of the mind, the smells, the sounds, the temperature of the place in which the writer is lodged; it feeds on all these things as it drifts from one thing to another; it ruminates. It pays very close attention to its own inclinations, both physical and mental, it retreats further and further inside itself, precisely in order to gather itself for a series of excursions, a succession of forays, that carry it as far as possible from its point of origin, almost to the point of no return, before feeling its way back again, more by homing instinct than by design. This recoiling movement that governs the writing and reading of the text, setting in motion the reader's attentiveness, keeping it afloat but seeming to lead it astray, off course, before drawing it back again to the author's mind from which its itinerary has derived, is implicit in the spatial arrangements of the *Essais'* scene of writing, the arrangements that Montaigne put in place to imitate in his provincial French chateau the conditions of a Renaissance *studiolo* – his library in a tower:

> When at home, I turn aside a little more often to my library, from which at one sweep I command a view of my household. I am over the entrance, and see below me my garden, my farmyard, my courtyard, and into most of the parts of my house. There I leaf through now one book, now another, without order and without plan, by disconnected fragments. One moment I muse, another moment I set down or dictate, walking back and forth, these fancies of mine that you see here.
>
> It is on the third floor of a tower; the first is my chapel, the second a bedroom and dressing room, where I often sleep in order to be alone. Above it is a great wardrobe. In the past it was the most useless place in my house. In my library I spend most of the days of my life, and most of the hours of the day. I am never there at night. Adjoining it is a rather elegant little room, in which a fire may be laid in winter, very pleasantly lighted by a window. And if I feared the trouble no more than the expense, the trouble that drives me from all business, I could easily add on to each side a gallery a hundred paces long and twelve wide, on the same level, having found all the walls raised, for

another purpose, to the necessary height. Every place of retirement requires a place to walk. My thoughts fall asleep if I make them sit down. My mind will not budge unless my legs move it. Those who study without a book are all in the same boat.

The shape of my library is round, the only flat side being the part needed for my table and chair; and curving round me it presents at a glance all my books, arranged in five rows of shelves on all sides. It offers rich and free views in three directions, and sixteen paces of free space in diameter. (Michel de Montaigne, 'Of Three Kinds of Association', 1585–88)

His tower gives Montaigne solitude, exclusiveness, the freedom to be himself, answerable to no one else; it gives him containment, concentration, the opportunity to distil himself and his thoughts; it gives him a vantage point, a commanding position from which he can see in almost every direction and over great distances; and it gives him time, a means of exit from the time of 'business' and entry into the time of the mind; time in which to imagine the construction of new buildings and time in which to realise the constructions of the imagination. Montaigne's reflections on his tower merge with his observations on his own writing. The compactness of the tower, its microcosmic character, its radial design and its circular library that epitomises the knowledge of the world, such that a few paces in any direction take its user across centuries of time and the geography of the known world, all these features of the place in which Montaigne sits down to write correspond to the organising principles of the essay, with its small compass, its self-containment, its telescopic enlargement of the small detail, and the exceptional freedom it grants to wander at will in any direction, and in any dimension.

Its informality has helped to give the impression that the essay is among the most modest of genres, but its conceptual scope permits it to be one of the most ambitious, the most extravagant.

Montaigne's writing lays down a template for the essay which has remained crucial to its subsequent development. It is formally and conceptually a niche in time and space, an insignificant interval when seen from outside, that once entered begins to expand, seemingly beyond natural limits, and sending probes into unknown territory. It is a place that you withdraw to on your own, a place that you make your own, and that seems to be right inside you; an interior that you look out from. Sooner or later the whole world goes past; it is a 'place of retirement' that is also 'a place to walk'. Elsewhere in the same text, Montaigne encapsulates the contrariness of the essay, its paradoxical ability to open outwards while seeming to fold inwards, its subtle reversal of the magnetic poles of self-communing and a sort of communicative abandon: 'Solitude of place, to tell the truth, rather makes me stretch and expand outward; I throw myself into affairs of state and into the world more readily when I am alone.'

But in many ways, Montaigne's work is also more radical than that of the vast majority of his followers, in that it cultivates an allergic resistance to the conclusive, the legislative, the incontrovertible. The habitual brevity and density of the essay have often fostered a weakness for trying to accomplish the impossible, the rendering down of an already very concentrated passage of thought into a single point. It is the minimal forms of literature that have most often succumbed to the maxim. Take the case of Sir Francis Bacon, the first writer in English to publish a series of texts under the title of 'Essays'. Bacon's writing gravitates almost automatically towards the sententious. It is a machine for the manufacture of *pensa*, of medicinal thoughts in pill-form, salutary pronouncements, each one the end product of a forensic procedure seeking to adjudicate between prescriptions for the best course in life. Montaigne avoids the shape, texture, weight and odour of the Great Thought, and if he ever seems to have it within reach in one sentence, it has slipped through his fingers in the next. The more he wrote, the less satisfied he became by the rounding off, the trimming and packaging of thoughts, the more fascinated he became by the brittleness and elusiveness of the process of thinking. If the freedom of the essay has meant that the essayist is all too often smitten by the higher purpose of his own thoughts, for Montaigne, true freedom of thought consists in thinking to no purpose.

Montaigne's tower is justly celebrated; like few other writers' houses it feels like the integument of a writing practice to which it is joined directly, organically. Montaigne returns to it every day, just as he handles the essay on a daily basis, without expectation, without a sense of occasion, since the occasions for writing are usually commonplace ones; like the tower, the essay absorbs the full range of different kinds of information from the outside world; it feeds on variety, thrives on the miscellaneous, on principle, and without prejudice, bearing out its author's famous claim, inscribed on his library ceiling, 'nothing human is foreign to me'. Like the tower, the essay functions ahead of its time like a kind of *camera obscura* for the projection of ideas, bringing closer and making clear the movement of thought, its surges and hesitations, its branching off in different directions, its arrivals and departures, its errors. It is an interior whose sole purpose is the manner of its linkage to the outside world. The tower is the focus of the surrounding countryside; the library is the conceptual heart of the tower; and Montaigne's body, sitting, getting up, walking a few paces, turning around, is the nerve-centre for the whole operation...

2012

Vacant History

At Dover, Matthew Arnold turned to Sophocles from a cold latitude: 'this distant northern sea'. He spoke from a familiar place as if from a great distance, although it was really his own times that seemed remote. Above the beach, a faded newsprint copy of his poem is fixed to the wall of a terraced house. The owner of the house, on the basis of no evidence whatsoever, plays host to an idea that Arnold wrote the poem in one of his rooms. The poem imagines the world not as the threshold between dream and reality, but as a perilous brink between dream and nightmare. The ghost of Arnold's idea – a self-haunting reverie – isn't knocking around in the cellarage or the wardrobes at the foot of the cliffs, but has a strange afterlife higher up, in the fragile archaeology of war lying scattered around on the brink of the chalk.

Here is the true vantage point for the darkling plain, the bomber's moon and ship-infested seas; here is where one imagines most clearly the withdrawal of dream and advance of nightmare; here perhaps the melancholy ebb and flow of military thinking, the prolonged echo of Arnold's ignorant armies, forever clashing by night.

The ruins on the Langdon site were built between 1884 and 1885 to house convict labour. The prisoners were earmarked for the construction of a new Admiralty harbour, but all they did was sew mailbags and chop firewood. In 1901, the name and function of the site changed to Dover

Military Prison. Expansion over the following year turned it into the biggest military jail in the country.

In the same year, the Langdon Battery was installed nearby, housing three enormous 9.2 inch guns. They were so long at 37 feet and so heavy at 27 tons that transporting them through the streets of the town proved impossible, and the monster barrels had to be rolled over the fields, for a distance of one mile. They saw action in the First World War but their main use was as a threat to shipping. They could not repulse the German Zeppelins, calling for quick-response anti-aircraft fire. According to the Langdon Fort Record Book, the Zeppelin threat was frequent and the airships were not deterred by AA fire, often cheating the gunners' best efforts. Despite their size, they frustrated attempts to bring them down, even when crippled. On 9 August 1915, a Zeppelin that had dropped bombs on Dover harbour was severely damaged by fire from the battery, but rather than plunge to earth or water, it 'rose and disappeared in cloud'.

The garrison saw no action for years at a time; their lives were captive to a gunboat diplomacy, they rusted for an oiled machine. Internment was what happened here, if not always in name then certainly in nature. They waited, and even when war obliged they waited some more. Langdon became a freeze-frame transit camp, the point of departure for troops heading to France, but departure was delayed: delay became the new marching orders; the marching orders rose and disappeared in cloud.

They waited and the buildings started to fall down. The Infirmary block lasted longest, acting as a Sergeant's Mess in World War Two, ending as a prisoner-of-war camp. The white cliffs, symbolic front line against German invasion, acquired half a millimetre of irony in history's reverse topping-out ceremony: five hundred metres of calcium

carbonate were surmounted by a thin crust of desponden-
cy, the sedimented longings of young-old Germans with
only one thing in mind: repatriation. Airborne seeds of
comfrey, hawkweed, kidney vetch, greater knapweed, this-
tledown, came and went. Loose rubble was embedded in
moss, moss was embedded in rubble. Voices from the port
carried up on the wind, English voices flawed into German
by gusts of yearning. The waves drew back like thoughts of
home receding into the past.

Langdon distils more waiting time into every cubic
inch of downland turf, and more concentrated desire for
elsewhere, than any other place on the English shoreline.
There is almost no here and now at Langdon. Its own his-
tory is a vapour into which past and future alike disappear.
If England is rooted in the imagining of its chalk bulwark,
then England is as chimerical as a blue bird over the white
cliffs. This member of the thrush family is native only to
the Americas. The librettist, Nat Burton, sang of the dis-
tant Kentish coast he had never seen, as if from long ac-
quaintance. Dovorians now join in the chorus, frequent
flyers over this dilapidating stage-set, riding the thermals
of port-mythology and homesickness by proxy.

2013

Underworld

When the heroine of Raymond Queneau's novel *Zazie dans
le Metro* arrives in Paris for the weekend, her sole desire is
to travel on the Metro. But the railway workers are on strike
and the entire system is closed for the duration of her visit,
only starting up again on the verge of her return to the
country. Although Zazie is from the rural hinterland, she

is no ingénue, and in fact the degree of her worldliness is shocking to all the residents of Paris she has any dealings with. Her mere presence in the city seems to catalyse a whole series of misadventures, transgressions, thefts, confidence tricks, traffic accidents and violent assaults. She becomes the mobile epicentre of urban lawlessness, and her strong, even passionate, identification with the Metro suggests that her irresistible energy and unruliness are somehow expressing a side to Paris that is only with difficulty kept under wraps, kept under control, or simply kept under. In the final episode of the novel, Zazie, along with her uncle and aunt and two sidekicks (plus a jaded parrot), escape from approaching ranks of armed police through the cellar of a brasserie, which connects with a sewer, which connects in turn with the Metro: 'A bit further on they crossed the threshold of another little door and found themselves in a corridor lined with glazed bricks, still dark and deserted.'[44]

This subterranean realm, which allows the team of carnivalesque characters to elude the grasp of the authorities, consists of an interlocking series of tunnels, mostly utilising the old stone quarries beneath the streets of Paris, and combining the underground railways with the sewers and catacombs. In Queneau's account, one system leaks into another, in a series of assimilations. But what these fugitives from the law are evading is in its turn equally protean and deceptive. The menacing squads of police are under the control of 'Haroun al Rations', a master of disguise who has assumed several different names and appearances over the course of the narrative, and who has been suspected by everyone else of being the most disreputable, the

44 Raymond Queneau, *Zazie in the Metro*, translated by Barbara Wright (London:Penguin Books, 2000), p.154.

most perverted, the most unredeemable character of all, as well as literally the most shifty. The two sides of Paris are seen to be almost interchangeable. Queneau's apparently high-spirited fable is in fact a quite savage reminder of the temporarily obscured, diplomatically neglected, history of Paris as an unparalleled centre of violence. Even the briefest of visits to the Musée Carnavalet, the museum of the history of Paris, will impress on the visitor the sheer frequency of desperate insurrections and ferocious acts of repression punctuating the history of the one hundred and seventy years before publication of *Zazie dans le Metro*.

Queneau lulls the reader into an acceptance of violence as slapstick, as pure spectacle, as a stimulus to humour in the same way that his linguistic violence, his cutting and splicing of different items of vocabulary, contributes to the overall comic atmosphere of the book. But all this changes in the penultimate chapter, when the illusion that violence can be entertaining and harmless is suddenly and brutally removed:

> Stepping over the pile of the crestfallen who constituted a sort of barricade in front of the entrance to the Queen of the Night, the widow Mouaque showed signs of intending to throw herself on the assailants who were advancing with deliberation and precision. A good fistful of tommy-gun bullets cut short this tentative. The widow Mouaque, holding her guts in her hands, collapsed.[45]

The description of the pile of bodies, of those who have been knocked-out in a bar-fight, is transformed from a scene in an animated film to something genuinely chilling by the use of the word 'barricade', evoking all the piles

---

45 Ibid, pp.152–3.

of real bodies left in the streets after the failed uprisings of the nineteenth century. And the apparent transformation of the 'gentle' Marceline, the only character not made the butt of others' jokes, into the anonymous lamp-bearer, who swiftly and efficiently conducts the others to safety at the end, suggests irresistibly a previous role in the metaphorical 'underground', the resistance movement of the Second World War:

> 'Tell me what happened.'
> 'This isn't the moment.'
> The lights came on.
> 'There you are,' said the other gently. 'The metro's working again. You, Gridoux take the Etoile line, and you, Turandot, the Bastille line.'[46]

Marceline's dispatch and intimate knowledge of underground spaces is reminiscent of accounts of resistance methods employed from one end of Europe to the other during the Second World War.[47]

But what of the choice of Zazie, the pubescent relative from the provinces, as the heroine of this narrative; what buried history is uncovered by her participation in its events? Consumers of popular Parisian culture from the mid-nineteenth century onwards could not fail to be aware of the figure of the *apache*, the abandoned, feral child, who roamed the streets in gangs, surviving through a combination of begging, stealing, assault and even murder. The cocky, amusingly precocious *apache* is a figure of myth, but

---

46 Ibid, pp.154–5.
47 See for example, Andrzej Wajda's film *Kanal* for the use of sewers by the Polish resistance movement.

behind the myth lies a miserable social history of child destitution. By 1848, there were no fewer than 130,000 abandoned children on the streets of Paris.[48] The scale of parental neglect was unprecedented, but the children visible on the streets represented only half the story, since even larger numbers of children were farmed out to rural wet-nurses. In 1866, half the children born in the city (around 25,000) were sent away from home to be cared for in this fashion. Many were not cared for at all, but allowed to sicken and die; some were murdered. Either way, large numbers of parents did not expect their children ever to return as burdens on the household income. Zazie, more Parisian than the Parisians themselves, an unsettling mixture of cynicism and innocence, equipped with more survival tactics than the adults around her, represents the return of the rusticated child to the streets of Paris. And her blind and unshakeable attachment to the very idea of the Metro suggests an equivalence between the physical underground and the undisclosed secrets of Parisian social psychology. Underground is where the Metro sits side by side with fear and shame in the psychopathology of modern life. Underground are resources that can be marshalled to undermine the order, efficiency and credibility of institutional control.

2013

---

48 Gregor Dallas, *Metrostop Paris* (2008) p.26.

The Dream of the Rood

The two figures of Mary and John, revealed in a beam of torchlight, are arcing away from the figure of Christ like a pair of strung longbows; Mary curving away to the left, John to the right. But the leading edge of each of these bow-shapes is the outline of gathered drapery falling into complex folds. Mary's right leg – the one nearest the viewer – is not planted solidly on the earth; it is weightless and curving, as if plied by the wind.

Her right hand clasps the left at an impossible angle. The left palm is bent backwards, away from the appalling fact, yet it repeats the angle of St John's right hand. He gestures towards the suffering of Christ, while she turns away, the dramatic slant of her fingers a literal index of her flinching away from the unbearable.

Mary's right leg also flexes in a recoil, while John's left leg inclines towards the object of empathy; yet his eye is seeking out the viewer, while her eye is fixed on what has shocked her so much.

The Christ figure is both an emblem of pain and an elegant displacement of pain, the two sinuous curves formed by upper and lower body implying the condition of grace that will outlive this episode. Christ's head is encircled not simply with thorns, but with a blue fillet that intensifies the powdery duck egg blues and greens of the background, an expanse of heavenly luminescence above a barely acknowledged strip of earth.

This wall-painting, almost a line drawing applied with fine brush, is modest in size but overpowering in expression. It can be found on the badly lit east chancel wall of the church of St Mary, Brent Eleigh. This well-preserved but unassuming building in an obscure part of Suffolk houses a masterpiece. The name of the village proclaims an event – conflagration ('brent' means 'burnt') – that would have prompted renovation and the skimming of a fresh layer of plaster above the high altar.

The hypothetical rescue operation is the most likely scenario for the commissioning of a small but definitive representation of the church's patron saint; at some point between 1280 and 1330, a visiting specialist would have spent a couple of hours plying his stock in trade, but at a certain stage of this process he would have realised that time and place had fallen away, that a routine depiction of transcendence had managed to transcend its brief; wherever this imagery recurred, it would only work if it managed to convince the viewer it might be the prime instance of its subject matter, its quintessential expression. The more obscure the place – the more local its reality – the more completely it would be translated into universal meaning. At the same time, the narrower the viewer's experience of the world, the greater the force of gravity exerted in that world – in every one of its local details.

At Brent Eleigh, these details are still observable in the surrounding landscape. The most direct route from Lavenham is along paths set with thorn-trees and oaks. In summer, the tower of Lavenham church is seen breasting the high fields of grain, its pale stone catching the sun, its white and red flag of St George stiff like a medieval pennant in the breeze. The wind rolls through everything, far and near: in the instant shiver of the poplars, in the leisurely swaying of the ash. Only the low-lying clover is motionless. The light glances through a field of barley and turns the oak leaves into photograms, each leaf bearing the x-ray shadows of other leaves behind it. In winter, when the quince is still on the branch, the way is through snow-bound-fields under a snow-heavy sky. There are stew ponds each with a thick roof of ice, and sloes to harvest with freezing cold hands.

Mary's hair is loose on both shoulders; her skirt and cloak fall to the ground and form rolls as stiff as crepe paper. The four wrists of Mary and John all point to the left, the direction in which Christ's head is inclined. There is nothing to distinguish the style of their garments, one from another, nothing to distinguish gender except hair dressing.

Christ's crown of thorns is both a torqued decoration and cruel band made from rose stem or bramble. The disposition of the holy body expresses both atrocity and finesse at one and the same time. The arms, thighs and chest are powerful, the slim waist almost svelte. With both Mary and John, the looping of cloth between shoulder and waist frames and focuses the action of their hands.

There is nothing but cerulean vacancy behind the three figures. The press of the crowd, the jostling to and fro, the cacophony of jeers, laments, prayers – all has melted away. For John and Mary, there is no one there but Christ and themselves.

In the figure of John, even the small muscles of the right-hand palm are defined. He is a little taller than Mary, who is bent backwards out of true slightly more than he is. Only the cross is straight and unyielding: a tree dreaming of continued growth ever upwards, breathing in another world entirely, another quality of light and air.

2014

Doris Salcedo and the Philosophy of Furniture

Beds, chairs, tables, doors, dressers, cabinets are not to be found in the work of Doris Salcedo, but there is a continual and compulsive production of un-beds, un-chairs, un-tables and other kinds of un-furniture, that both remember and dis-member the commonest, the most generic articles of furniture in daily use. My use of the 'un' prefix is intended to catch an echo of George Bataille's concept of 'l'Informe' – the formless – as defined in the 'Critical Dictionary' he included in the *Documents* project he edited in 1929–30: 'A dictionary would begin from the point at which it no longer rendered the meanings of words but rather their tasks. Thus *formless* is not only an adjective with a given meaning but a term which declassifies, generally requiring that each thing take on a form.'[49] Salcedo's frequent practice of dismembering furniture and breaking it down into sections, then mismatching the sections to create furniture equivalents of the *exquisite corpse*, threatens to remove meaning from objects by declassifying them; wrenching them out of one form without supplying another, since the hybrid condition they end up in leaves them suspended in a state of formal hesitation.

The specific content of Salcedo's work requires us to think of formlessness in relation to homelessness. Her sculptures are homeless three times over, whose first home is the class of objects to which they should conform, and whose second home is the domestic setting where such objects are always found. After their deformation at the hands of Salcedo, these relics of furniture are transplanted to the art gallery, where

49 Georges Bataille, 'Formless', in *Documents*, Vol.1, no.7. (December, 1929), translated by Dominic Faccini, in *October*, Vol.60 (Spring, 1992), p.27.

at first glance they seem out of place, even despite the rapidity with which we adjust to admit the anomalous and the untimely to the scenes of contemporary art. Salcedo's works are perhaps even more definitively out of time than they are out of place. They include found materials imprinted by time; indeed, positively encompassed by it; but different materials react differently to the passing of time – some are more impressionable than others – and the grafting of one onto another may produce temporal bewilderment. Time is of the essence in all her work, such that the amount and quality of time the viewer devotes to it is measured against the different timescales involved in its composition: both the sedimented time attached to its various materials and the metamorphic time of its fabrication.

It is worth asking, what is the nature of the time that is attached to these objects? They come to us, dragging behind them various histories of attention, but chiefly the knowledge that the bulk of their materials have been subject in the past to a form of contemplation different to how we see them in the present. For the most part, the materials salvaged from items of furniture have belonged to everyday objects so familiar, so taken for granted, that the only form of attention we can muster on their behalf is that of habitual recognition; either that, or we are likely to overlook them entirely. At the most, our intimacy with their shapes and surfaces, with their look and feel, is so repetitious in character that no single moment of their presence in our lives, no particular memory of them, is likely to stand out. When they have been the setting for crises or turning points, our minds push them into the background.

Our furniture accompanies us more frequently than practically any other object in our passage through time. And we may give it a lifetime's use; even several lifetimes' use. Chairs and tables, beds, chests and dressers are passed down through generations; we all possess objects that have outlived other lives, perhaps several lives. One thing is certain: our furniture will outlive us.

And the forms of these objects have lasted much longer. What has changed less than the form of a chair in the last four thousand years; of a table, a bed, a bath, a door, a dresser? The phenomenology that centres on these objects: the attitude of a seated body towards a table; the sequence of muscular actions we undergo to sit and then lie on a bed; the slight resistance of an opening door; none of this has altered very much in thousands of years.

In this context, Salcedo's sabotage of the object, her breaking and re-setting of its materials, like bones that have to be splinted – and there are bones attached to wood and cement in several Salcedo works – is not even primarily a physical break, the sign of an event in space, a change in the substance of the object, but more importantly a temporal event, that cleaves apart the space of the living from that of the dead. The damaged object has no further use to the living, and belongs with the departed.

This is irresistibly reminiscent of the ancient funerary practice of burying the dead with broken grave goods, including broken furniture. An unbroken table speaks to the living of the experience of living, even during its posthumous existence beyond the death of its first owner. A broken table cannot resume its place among the living, and so belongs with the dead. So much of Salcedo's work speaks to the living about the dead, while it also speaks to the dead about the mindfulness of those who have survived them.

I have always sensed this obligation of mindfulness in my first-hand observation of Salcedo's work on several occasions during the last ten years, but I felt possessed by it during a period of three months over the summer of 2013, when I curated an exhibition that had at its moral and political and aesthetic centre a micro-version of Salcedo's major installation *Plegaria Muda*. This work has multiple units, but the main constituent of each unit is a pair of wooden tables. A significant number of the hybrid objects in Salcedo's work of the last two decades have utilised sets of chairs and tables. This powerful use of metonymy – employing motifs that do not merely symbolise social relationships but which are materially involved in them – provides the most concise expression of the bond between the individual and the social unit. Single chairs evoke and stand in for single persons, while their being placed around a table is a primary instance of what draws the individual into the social group. In the work from this period, strange versions of both chairs and tables were forced into unnatural and disturbing combinations.

In *Plegaria Muda* we are faced with a mass of tables and a repetition of elements, and yet each unit of paired tables, both joined and separated by a layer of earth, is individuated by the unpredictable growth pattern of grass seedlings sown into the earth. The contradictory structure of the installation echoes the tension between commemoration and anonymity that has always complicated the social psychology of cenotaphs and graves of unknown soldiers. Describing Colombia as the country of 'unburied death', she conceives of her work as a demarcated space for symbolic burial [and states]: 'Reyes Mate writes that each murder generates an absence in our lives and demands that we take responsibility for the absent, since the only way they can exist is within us, in the process of living out our grief.' Recognising that process of interiorisation as inevitable and unspeakable, *Plegaria Muda* – the title means 'mute prayer' – nonetheless proposes to restore such deaths to the sphere of the human, to the mute eloquence of the objects and relationships from which they were so violently wrenched.

In our installation, in the Romanesque chapel at the heart of the medieval buildings of Jesus College, Cambridge, where I am curator, we had five units of *Plegaria Muda*, five pairs of tables and layers of earth to arrange within the stone built-rectangle of a transept of the chapel. The space was empty apart from medieval grave slabs in the floor and memorial slabs on the wall – a reticent space but one which already spoke quietly of commemorative practice. On the day of the installation we had not yet received a floor-plan from Doris's studio and were short of time before the opening. We decided to try out an arrangement of the five units and slowly but surely found one that seemed to lock into place. We had just finished when the floor-plan came through. Extraordinarily, four of the five units were exactly where Doris wanted them, and the fifth was only one table's length away from where it needed to be. This produced a measure of complacency, always unwise in curation. I visited the installation several times during the first week, feeling more and more that everything about it was just right. Then the grass started to die, and panic – my panic – set in. The fabulous stained glass windows that were all the work of Edward Burne-Jones were not admitting enough light. It wasn't that I was worried Doris might be angry (though I was, a little) it was more an anxiety that the underlying purpose of the work was not being served, that the obligation on me was becoming less and less curatorial, more and more ethical: I had to keep alive something that was dying, and by so doing, preserve that margin of the work that was addressed more importantly to the dead than to the living. (We saved the grass – we put a stadium's worth of lamps on it every night and watered it as if it was the only green thing in the whole of the east of England.)

Those paired tables are almost identical to one another, but while one achieves the function all tables have for the living, the other denies and reverses it. They are mirror images of one another, not just in their physical disposition and visual aspect, but in their fitness for purpose. Like the houses for the dead constructed during the Neolithic, which duplicate the architecture, furniture and internal arrangements of houses for the living, they are exact counterparts in everything but use. Our houses are full of furniture, but we no longer build replicas of them for the dead – instead we have art galleries, where we see the paraphernalia of our daily lives undergo metamorphosis into another state.

So much of Salcedo's earlier work involves a breaking and grafting, dividing and fusing of different objects and materials with an assertiveness that makes the understated discrepancies of *Plegaria Muda's* furniture assemblages seem initially much less disturbing. But the latter's simple inversions of form are more systematic and more insidious. The aesthetic symmetry of their mirrored tables threatens semantic disorder on the scale envisaged by Mary Douglas's reflections on matter that is out of place, in *Purity and Danger*:

'Order implies restriction: from all possible materials, a limited selection has been made and from all possible relations a limited set has been used. So disorder is by implication unlimited, no pattern has been realised in it, but its potential for patterning is indefinite. This is why, though we seek to create order, we do not simply condemn disorder. We recognise that it is destructive to existing patterns; also that it has potentiality. It symbolises both danger and power.'[50]

---

50 Mary Douglas, *Purity and Danger: An Analysis of Concepts of Pollution and Taboo* (Routledge & Kegan Paul, 1966), p. 94.

The mirrored tables of *Plegaria Muda* seem perhaps too logical in their inversions of order: seen in isolation, the paired gestures are almost too perfectly synchronised. But taken together, their multiple misalignments produce a chain-reaction of disorder, a ricochet-effect of entropy, an unravelling of pattern wherever we look.

The dead exist in our mindfulness about them, a mindfulness that often takes shape as a search for closure, a search for the right pattern; but there is no finality in such patterns, and our mindfulness about the dead is an ever-renewed pattern-making that never settles into order; we say we want the dead to find rest, but it is only a form of words to bring comfort to the living; and the most adequate form of attention towards the dead is to keep them in mind, restlessly alive.

I used the word metamorphosis earlier to describe what happens when art takes hold of the everyday and changes the kind of attention we pay towards it, selecting articles of everyday use that we are accustomed to push into the back of our minds, in order to bring them into focus, and with them, the value of what they make possible: the condition of being fully human. We mark the stages of our induction into the conventional range of experiences making up that condition with rites of passage, more or less ostentatious performances of growth through transition. But there are certain artists who propose that these rites are joined end to end, in a condition of slow and continuous transition whose progress and value we are hardly aware of. These artists include Salcedo, and they include Kafka.

Kafka's story *Die Verwandlung*, usually translated as *Metamorphosis* takes as its premise an overnight transformation from the human condition to something quite alien: that of a beetle or cockroach. But the process by which Gregor Samsa loses his sense of belonging to a family, a social and economic structure, a species, is slow and continuous throughout the narrative; the story puts into reverse the usual process by which the individual becomes integrated into a gender role, family membership, social identity, and it marks the significance of the ever loosening hold that these things have on Gregor's awareness of existence through what happens to the furniture.

It is only when his mother and sister decide to remove the furniture from his room that Gregor understands what it means to cease to be human: 'Did he really want his warm room, so comfortably fitted with old family furniture, to be turned into a naked den in which he would certainly be able to crawl unhampered in all directions but at the price of shedding simultaneously all recollection of his human background? [...] They were clearing his room out; taking away everything he loved; the chest in which he kept his fret saw and other tools was already dragged off; they were now loosening the writing desk at which he had done all his homework when he was at the commercial academy, at the grammar school before that, and yes, even at the primary school [...] And so he rushed out [...]'[51] The furniture is nothing more nor less than an instrument of sedimented time and experience. The complete undoing of Gregor's belief in his own humanity is marked by his ultimate indifference when the furniture in his room is eventually replaced by refuse and bric-a-brac.

The *Metamorphosis* dates from 1915; one year earlier Kafka describes in a letter a shopping expedition made with his then fiancée Felice Bauer:

---

51 Franz Kafka, 'Metamorphosis', in *Collected Stories*, translated by Willa and Edwin Muir (New York: Knopf, 1993), pp.104–6.

We went shopping in Prague for furniture for a Prague official. Heavy furniture that looked as though it could never be removed once it was in place. Its solidity is exactly what you liked most about it. My chest felt crushed by the sideboard; it was a perfect tombstone or a monument to the life of an official in Prague. If a funeral bell had begun to chime anywhere in the distance while we were in the furniture store, it would not have been inappropriate.'[52]

What Kafka is effectively saying here is that we went shopping – not for me, or for you, or for the both of us, but for an idea of existence, the existence of a 'Prague official', which I do not want. The metamorphosis from unmarried to married man is identified with another rite of passage, between life and death, in which Kafka's sense of self will be buried in his identity as a Prague 'official'. The transformation is marked by the threat of being oppressed and overwhelmed by the wrong kind of furniture: a tombstone that is masquerading as a sideboard.

Beckett is another writer – one that we know is important to Salcedo – whose work gives to furniture a crucial role in measuring the dimensions of human relationships in the very process of their withdrawal. His notebooks are stuffed full of descriptions of furniture that have all been disposed of before publication in one account after another of the remorseless exfoliation of human contact. What sticks of furniture remain become the focus of obsessive routines that are progressively isolating in effect.

I think Salcedo is using furniture in her work to make it ask questions of us that are very similar to the questions asked by Beckett and Kafka. In Kafka's fragmentary narrative 'Home-Coming', a prodigal son is unable to return

---

52 Reinar Stach, *Kafka: The Decisive Years*, p.429.

home, unable to be reintegrated into family life, because he cannot come to terms with the furniture, cannot hear what it is saying to him: 'My father's house it is, but each object stands cold beside the next, as though preoccupied with its own affairs, which I have partly forgotten, partly never known. What use can I be to them, what do I mean to them?'[53] Leaving home and returning home are, of course, important rites of passage. What Salcedo's furniture-based sculptures are doing is not making us ask, what use are these works to me, what do they mean to me? but what use can I be them, what do I mean to them? They are works that have been rendered formless with legendary care and precision; they use materials that have been rendered homeless on purpose and on principle; they come to us bringing all kinds of sedimented meanings that have been metamorphosed in the processes of fabrication and installation; and they place on us an obligation to be mindful of the very real, historical experiences that they have been drawn from.

2015

Steve McQueen's Static and the State We're In

McQueen's Static circles around more than just the Statue of Liberty, which is one of the most familiar icons of all time, yet one whose meanings have been anything but static in the almost one hundred and fifty years since first conception. The name chosen for McQueen's film is ironic in respect of the constant shifting of position between the original intentions of the French abolitionist activist

53 Ibid, p.415.

Laboulaye, the broad appeal of the statue's national symbolism, fostered by American politicians, and the spontaneous perceptions of immigrants on arrival at Ellis Island. As a black artist, McQueen will surely have registered the deriding of the statue's received meanings by the African American press on the occasion of its dedication in 1886. And in the one hundred and thirty years since then, it has been impossible to stabilise or consolidate the perceptions of artists and writers – especially poets – whose very active conscriptions have turned the statue into a virtual monument of disunity. This essay will concentrate on the writing strategies of Hart Crane and Samuel Beckett that offer especially powerful models for thinking about and representing the evasive symbolism of the Statue of Liberty, whose presence on the North American shoreline comes to resemble that of a modern Proteus.

Even materially, the statue has undergone constant change. It existed for many years as just a part of itself – the arm holding the torch – exhibited separately in Philadelphia in 1876. The head came next, also as a separate entity, exhibited in Paris in 1878. When the construction of the whole figure was underway, the plan to clothe a 150ft-high brick pier in copper sheeting was exchanged for that of an iron scaffold that would be more flexible in high winds. The statue itself has never actually stood still; by the 1980s the point of one of the sunrays projecting from its crown was seen to be sawing through the arm as its rocking motion grew more pronounced. It is possible to move around inside the statue and to share its own perspective on the world, but not always: public access has been withdrawn for long periods of time, especially after the events of 9/11 and the re-examination of ideas of liberty and licence, and how variously they can be understood. McQueen's film was made towards the end of a period of closure, lasting from 2001 to 2009, when the statue could only be experienced at a distance.

In this context, the bird's eye view of the statue shared by McQueen's camera cannot avoid an association with the kinds of surveillance manoeuvres performed routinely by police helicopters. The statue is more than just a symbol of liberty, a vehicle for the idea of a society founded on the principle of individual rights, it is also a metonym for the condition in which that society actually exists, subject to certain limitations on its freedom of movement. In McQueen's film, liberty itself is being shadowed and monitored like a suspect – as well it might be, since absolute liberty is a serious threat to the state.

Static hovers obsessively over the question of how much or how little the reduction of liberty is justified; and in whose interest, finally, is a regime of control to be maintained? Of course, this question is sharpened by the realisation that the circling movement of the airborne camera is also that of the airliners whose mercilessly controlled collision with the Twin Towers was what triggered the introduction of emergency powers. We can understand the suspension of access to the Statue of Liberty as a practical measure, but the statue is not just an actual place but also an idea, a problematically constructed idea with a long history of controversy over its meanings, and it is therefore a site whose local reality is almost lost behind the global reputation it has acquired. The question of liberty is truly cornered by this film, which has no time or space for anything else, its brief span an epitome of the arbitrariness involved in any truncation of its scope.

'Static' is also a noun referring to the noise that interferes in the transmission of radio or telecommunications systems. The only noise we hear in McQueen's film of the same name is that of the helicopter engine that drowns out all other ambient sounds. The medium of aural representation is filled with the sound of its own apparatus, the helicopter being a necessary component in the mechanical system of filmmaking – as necessary as in a surveillance regime. Radical critique in the medium of film uses the same machinery as that of counter-terrorism. The output signal of independent film-making encounters feedback when its point of view, its style of documentation and its technical media all reproduce those of control systems. And *vice versa*: surveillance procedures can be foregrounded by independent film-making as key elements in the move to a social reality where an increased degree of control is accepted as normal; just part of the everyday routines of the modern state.

When it was first thought of, by the French anti-slavery campaigner Edouard Rene de Laboulaye, the statue was intended to celebrate the principle of freedom exemplified by the abolition of slavery in 1865. But it is now understood universally as a symbol of the open arms policy towards immigration that has prevailed for much of the history of the United States. The decisive factor in this respect has been poetry; in particular, the words of the sonnet 'The New Colossus' written by Emma Lazarus in 1883, when the statue was still under construction. As a figure welcoming new arrivals to the United States, the statue has become indissolubly linked to the phrasing of the sonnet's lines 10–12:

> Give me your tired, your poor,
> Your huddled masses yearning to breathe free,
> The wretched refuse of your teeming shore.

However, the poem was not in fact mounted on the pedestal of the statue until 1903, with word and image circling around one another for a period of twenty years before their relationship was literally cemented. The poem's title links the statue to yet another association that was certainly in the mind of its designer, Frédéric Auguste Bartholdi, who had proposed in the 1860s to build a lighthouse at the entrance of the Suez Canal amalgamating elements of two of the ancient Wonders of the World, the Pharos of Alexandria and the Colossus of Rhodes. The torch in the hand of the Statue of Liberty retains the association with a lighthouse beacon, while Lazarus's poem envisages the upraised arm of the statue holding a lamp to light the way to an open door. This scenario is behind Lazarus's appellation of the statue as 'Mother of Exiles', beckoning emigrants to their true home. However, the maternal element is absent from classical and Revolutionary French conceptions of Liberty as a virginal figure.

Subsequent poetry has changed the meanings that the sponsors and builders of the statue hoped to leave to posterity, but it has also given it a longer and longer anteriority by tracing the origins of its meanings in historical and mythological precedents. The passage of time occupied by the viewer of McQueen's film is enough to register the fact that what is being contemplated is always seen during a period of transition; is always undergoing some degree of semantic transformation – at times gradual and unspectacular; at other times, sudden and dramatic. But it is actually never static.

McQueen's practice in this film and other early works has been seen as non-narrative and therefore, almost by default, as poetic. Certainly, poetry has been described – most influentially by Roman Jakobson – as being organised primarily along a vertical rather than horizontal axis, consolidating its meanings not by means of the consequential unfolding of story, plot and hermeneutical progress, but through the amplification of figure, trope, consonance and

what we might call idea-rhymes. In this sense, the prog-
ress that is gained through reading a poem is not linear in
character, and might well be thought of in terms of cir-
cling round and round the same set of concerns in order to
augment and refine our awareness of them. Certainly, this
is the effect of reading the poetry of Hart Crane, whose
work returns several times to the Statue of Liberty, giv-
ing it an unusual depth of context, and a salutary ambigu-
ity. The most complete single statement of its potency as
a socio-political emblem for the historical significance of
American statehood is Crane's poem 'To Liberty':

> Out of the seagull cries and wind
> On this strange shore I build
> The virgin. They laugh to hear
> How I endow her, standing
> Hair mocked by the sea, her lover
> A dead sailor that knew
> Not even Helen's fame.
> Light the last torch in the wall,
> The sea wall. Bring her no robes yet.
> They have not seen her in this harbour;
> Eyes widely planted, clear, yet small.
> And must they overcome the fog,
> Or must we rend our dream?[54]

This poem written at some point in the late 1920s and un-
published during Crane's lifetime may have been left unfin-
ished. It is tempting to think that its thirteen lines might re-
flect an attempt to respond to Lazarus's fourteen line sonnet.
I quote it here because it draws symptomatically on other

54 Hart Crane, 'To Liberty', in *Complete Poems* (Newcastle upon
Tyne: Bloodaxe Books, 1984), p.162.

traditions of thought about American liberty than that now associated with interpretation of the statue since Lazarus's poem was affixed to it, both physically and ideologically. The most immediately striking difference is the identification of the figure as a virgin, since this forges a link with the earliest personification of America as Virginia, with the name given to the earliest settlement by Europeans denoting a land previously untouched, even though the first settlers would have known very rapidly that there was no basis in fact for such a claim. But the name stuck because the idea of the land as a *tabula rasa* was needed by Europeans wishing to fashion a way of life there that was a projection of the desires they had brought with them from the Old World. Crane insisted on the essential 'virginity' of America throughout his work, precisely because the experience of first landfall was repeated hundreds of times over with the arrival of each boatload of immigrants from elsewhere. America became the screen on which the immigrants would project their hopes and wishes for a fresh start. Crane's major work 'The Bridge 1930' begins ostensibly with an address to Brooklyn Bridge, but the address is deflected almost immediately by an acknowledgement of the Statue of Liberty, viewed across the harbour. The switching of attention is partly cognisant of the allure of the statue and what it represents to those seeing it for the first time, an allure conceived of precisely in terms of cinematically curated desires:

I think of cinemas, panoramic sleights
With multitudes bent towards some flashing scene
Never disclosed but hastened to again,
Foretold to other eyes on the same screen[55]

---

55 Hart Crane, 'To Brooklyn Bridge' in *Complete Poems*, ibid, p. 63.

America itself is being conceived of as a spectacle of illusions: fantasies of renewal and redemption – deceptive fictions for the most part, but necessary fictions all the same. The power of dreams is such that Crane imagines it detaining even the Statue of Liberty itself:

And Thee, across the harbour, silver paced
As though the sun took step of thee, yet left
Some motion ever unspent in thy stride, –
Implicitly thy freedom staying thee!

If we pause to ask ourselves the question, What does the Statue of Liberty think?, the answer is, according to Hart Crane, the same as every refugee who gazes on its face – it is 'stayed', which is to say that its desires are arrested, in a condition in which freedom can only ever be qualified. Every refugee knows that movement is the first condition of their freedom, but Crane observes and dwells on the fact that Liberty herself is in a pose of arrested movement: of stasis, in fact. The idea of Liberty literally outruns the reality.

Even more revealing and suggestive is Crane's opening address in the same poem, which is made not directly to Brooklyn Bridge, but to a seagull flying above it:

How many dawns, chill from his rippling rest
The seagull's wings shall dip and pivot him,
Shedding white rings of tumult, building high
Over the chained bay waters Liberty –

In defiance of the ideological version of freedom represented by the architecture of public statuary, the climbing motion of the seagull is 'building' towards an airborne expression of true freedom. There is an astonishing parallel here for the viewer of McQueen's film between the circular pattern of the 'white rings' left on the surface of the 'rippling' sea where the bird rests, as well as the circular pattern of its flight as it wheels ever higher above the harbour, and the circling manoeuvres of McQueen's helicopter as it traverses the same airspace. Crane underlines the natural freedom of the bird by insisting that the 'bay waters' under the jurisdiction of the Port Authority of New York are 'chained', in a deliberate and provocative allusion to the broken chain that lies at the feet of the Statue of Liberty as part of the work. By comparison with the seagull's unconditional freedom, the sculptural representation of a broken chain is no more than a rhetorical gesture, since the motion of the statue is impeded regardless. By juxtaposing Crane's gull with McQueen's helicopter, we can appreciate the full force of the latter's irony in tracing out a cinematic architecture with the flight paths of an authoritarian reaction to what, in 2009, seems an extenuation of political paranoia.

To return to the two verses of Crane's poem 'To Liberty', the second half of the first verse evokes the epic tradition that gave poetry real ideological power in the forging of nationality and statehood. The reference to Helen in connection with a 'dead sailor', alludes to the twin aftermaths of the Trojan War, in the story of Odysseus, who was to be turned into the archetypal exile for European culture, and the journey of Aeneas, departing from the ruins of Troy to found the state and future empire of Rome. Crane's sailor does not share either of these illustrious fates and is a reminder of the many unremembered refugees and exiles whose stories – and sometimes, whose lives – are simply lost. Crane's second verse insists on the lighting of torches for those who have not yet returned home or, more realistically, who have yet to reach their new 'home'. The outcome of all those anticipated journeys hangs in the balance, since it is too early to decide what 'robes' to wear, in expression of mourning or celebration, and Crane's virgin here seems to double for the widows whose part in the national story is given architectural expression in all the 'widows' walks' seen in houses along the coast of New England. The poem concludes with a set of alternatives which render ambivalent the advantages of seeing through or past 'fog' to ascertain a reality which might do no more than 'rend our dream', suggesting that Liberty is more of a dream than anything else, and that its insubstantiality must be recognised even if it is repeatedly embraced.

Of course, McQueen's film does not refer directly to these poems, but it works in comparable ways and elicits reflection on the same range of concerns. As a British-born artist of Grenadian and Trinidadian descent, McQueen is in a position to be especially sensitive to the fundamental challenges to a sense of identity that translocation involves, including the impossibility of fully replacing one idea of 'home' with another, as well as the advantages and disadvantages of exile. Among his own stated artistic influences, he has named Beckett with some frequency and has incorporated Beckett's own language into the titles of several of his films and exhibitions. He admires Beckett's economy of means, combining resonance with extreme concentration, and emulates the writer's carefully calculated reticence and obliqueness. But his work also overlaps many of Beckett's central concerns in its conceptual focus. Beckett is in many ways the exemplary writer as exile, going further than many in his use of a second language as chief means of expression for the majority of his works written after departure from Ireland. All of these works dwell obsessively on departure from home and on the locations and relationships left behind, insisting on exile, vagrancy and the necessity for increasing the distance between origin and destination, while always looping back psychologically to repetitions with variations of the same scenarios, revisiting past dreams of anticipated futures, and reviewing past decisions in order to recapture imagined alternatives. Beckett's abandonment of English to write in French reverses the priorities encountered by emigrants to the United States, but parallels their situation in having to remake the self through acclimatisation to the mindset and sensibility permitted by the host language. Part of the self is inevitably lost in translation. Beckett typically writes in French about a past Irish self originally constructed through the medium of English. For much of his career Beckett deployed a wry comedy to camouflage an unbearable degree of emotional damage and to convert this into a pretext for resilience, while in his late works there is a much more anaesthetic evenness of tone, suggesting an excessive degree of self-alienation.

But even in his late English works there is an obsession with the point of origin from which one is irrevocably removed, requiring a constant reassessment and redefinition of concepts of home, of the maternal and paternal, of the landscape that provided initial orientation in the world. A focal work for McQueen is the short play Not I, whose opening words 'Into this World' when transplanted to the filmmaker's world immediately relocate the Beckettian reference to birth to the settings of a twenty-first-century socio-political reality. McQueen was to use the phrase as the title of his show at the Thomas Dane Gallery in 2004. But the structure of Beckett's text, organised around key moments of uncertainty about the identity of the self, involves a compulsive circling around the experience of dislocation and disassociation that is reflected in the many-layered, concentric movements of McQueen's Static, a more detached and meditative work, but one which is never very far from a sense of political pressure, and touching incidentally on so many of the same threats, anxieties and lost illusions.

2016

The Prose Poem

One of the main points I want to make in this essay about the prose poem comes out of reading something which isn't a prose poem, but a passage from a novel. The novel is Dickens's *Great Expectations*, published in the weekly *All the Year Round* between 1 December 1860 and 3 August 1861, and the passage I'm interested in was published on 11 May 1861. It concerns one of the most momentous narrative junctures in the novel: momentous because it describes a protracted moment, but also because it records a life-changing experience. The experience is that of passing from a state of self-possession to that of being effectively the property of another, and it hinges on the management of time:

Alterations have been made in that part of the Temple since that time, and it has not now so lonely a character as it had then, nor is it so exposed to the river. We lived at the top of the last house, and the wind rushing up the river shook the house that night, like discharges of cannon, or breakings of a sea. When the rain came with it and dashed against the windows, I thought, raising my eyes to them as they rocked, that I might have fancied myself in a storm-beaten light-house. Occasionally, the smoke came rolling down the chimney as though it could not bear to go out into such a night; and when I set the doors open and looked down the staircase, the staircase lamps were blown out; and when

I shaded my face with my hands and looked through the black windows (opening them ever so little, was out of the question in the teeth of such wind and rain) I saw that the lamps in the court were blown out, and that the lamps on the bridges and the shore were shuddering, and that the coal fires in barges on the river were being carried away before the wind like red-hot splashes in the rain.

I read with my watch upon the table, purposing to close my book at eleven o'clock. As I shut it, Saint Paul's, and all the many church-clocks in the City – some leading, some accompanying, some following – struck that hour. The sound was curiously flawed by the wind; and I was listening, and thinking how the wind assailed and tore it, when I heard a footstep on the stair.[56]

The passage describes a spell of time, stepping out of the main narrative flow of the novel and setting up some boundaries that keep at bay the pace and rhythm of that flow, before stepping back into it with the sound of a literal step upon the stair. Pip, the narrator, is comfortably in control of his own timetable – he puts his own watch upon the table, and sets aside a precise amount of time for reading – but the comfort he takes from being able to choose the order of his life is about to be revealed as complacent and illusory, since the step upon the stair brings the knowledge that Magwitch has devised a completely different and conflicting schedule for Pip's sense of direction and purpose, completely altering his understanding of the relations between his past, present and future. This is the moment when one schedule is engulfed by the other, when several possible futures disappear. And this dramatic

56 Charles Dickens, *Great Expectations*, ed. Angus Calder (Harmondsworth: Penguin Books, 1965), pp.331–2.

change of time signature is backed by the striking of the hour at different times by different churches, disclosing a hinterland of different temporal measures, a multiplication of plans and frameworks for living, a plurality of different stories contained by the city, whose sheer volume and lack of coordination are overpowering to the solitary individual.

Pip himself emphasises his solitude; his actions reveal a desire for solitude, a need to retreat from interference. Dickens puts him on the *top* floor of the *last* house and makes him imagine, retrospectively, that it must be like dwelling in a lighthouse, in a living space whose confinement and remoteness from the rest of humanity is what makes it attractive; his rooms have windows, but they are all black; the buildings have lamps, but they have all gone out; there is no visual evidence of anyone else alive, or of any living thing, for that matter – only the fugitive gleams of a few primeval flares, 'red-hot splashes' being carried down the river as if on a flow of lava.

And in this physical and imaginative isolation – there is just Pip among the elements – the most appropriate action for Pip to perform is reading; he shuts out the disorientating spatial dimensions of the city, focusing on the small space of the book; and he shuts out the confused and confusing temporal dimensions of the city, by tethering the minutes and the hours to his own watch, and by entering the time of reading; what Pip is reading is another text than the one he is in, *Great Expectations*; and the kind of text he needs, even if he does not know it is what he wants, must be something like a prose poem.

Why do I say this? In 1860, during the year in which the serialisation of *Great Expectations* commenced, James Hogg published the last of his *Selections Grave and Gay from the Writings published and unpublished* of Thomas de Quincey.

It included De Quincey's essay 'On the Knocking at the Gate in *Macbeth*', which asks the reader to compare the effect of the knocking with the experience of being 'in a vast metropolis on the day when some great national idol was carried in funeral pomp to his grave', resulting in 'the silence and desertion of the streets' and 'the stagnation of ordinary business'. De Quincey then focuses on the relevant scene in *Macbeth* in terms that are strikingly close to those employed by Dickens in the passage from *Great Expectations* just given:

In order that a new world may step in, this world must for a time disappear. The murderers, and the murder, must be insulated – cut off by an immeasurable gulph from the ordinary tide and succession of human affairs – locked up and sequestered in some deep recess: we must be made sensible that the world of ordinary life is suddenly arrested – laid asleep – tranced – racked into a dread armistice: time must be annihilated; relation to things without abolished; and all must pass self-withdrawn into a deep syncope and suspension of earthly passion. Hence it is that when the deed is done – when the work of darkness is perfect, then the world of darkness passes away like a pageantry in the clouds: the knocking at the gate is heard; and it makes known audibly that the reaction has commenced: the human has made its reflux upon the fiendish: the pulses of life are beginning to beat again: and the re-establishment of the goings-on of the world in which we live, first makes us profoundly sensible of the awful parenthesis that had suspended them.[57]

57 Thomas de Quincey, 'On the Knocking at the Gate in *Macbeth*', in *Confessions of an English Opium-Eater, and other Writings* (Oxford: The World's Classics, 1985), pp.84–5.

De Quincey's emphasis on insulation, sequestration and deep recesses; his looping together of ideas of suspension, trance, syncope; and his breaking of the spell with the return of hearing and the insistence of the knocking that recalls the ordinary rhythm of time marked by the ticking of the clock or the chiming of the bell – reminding us also of the tremendous forward momentum of the dramatic action in *Macbeth* – all these features are at the centre of Dickens's passage written a few months after the book publication of the essay. But what is also at the centre of De Quincey's essay, but not mentioned, in fact effaced, is that the cessation of all the goings-on of the world in which we have to live, according to measures and rhythms imposed upon us by others, is occasioned not only by the work of darkness, but also – and for De Quincey especially – by the workings of opium: by its ability to estrange us from our familiar routines, surroundings, and relations, and even from our own bodies, imprinted with the actions and reactions of the habitual.

The syntactical structure of De Quincey's rendition of the trance is itself a performance of extenuation, of delay; of prevarication through paraphrase and revision; withholding the moment when the sentence completes itself and breaks the illusion. The text seems to be mesmerised by its own ability to spin things out – what Ruth apRoberts refers to in her essay on Biblical parallelism in English prose as 'self-exegesis'.[58]

At the same time that Dickens was working on *Great Expectations*, that other opium-eater, Baudelaire, was composing some of his most important prose poems. He did this while working simultaneously on his enthusiastic

---

58 Ruth apRoberts, 'Old Testament Poetry: the Translatable Structure', PMLA 92 (1977), pp.987–1004.

translations of De Quincey, whose work he was thoroughly familiar with. In 1862, the year following the publication of the Dickens passage we have just looked at, Baudelaire completed one of his most arresting *Petits Poèmes en prose*, 'La Chambre Double' ['The Twofold Room']. For the sake of convenience, I am giving this in the English translation by Francis Scarfe and shortening it to about half its total length. I don't think this shorter version seriously misrepresents the whole, and it amounts to something like a concertina version of the full text:

> A room just like a daydream, a truly spiritual room, in which the unmoving air is faintly tinged with rosiness and blue.
>
> In it the soul enjoys a bath of stillness, a bath scented with regret and desire. It has something of twilight about it, bluish and roseate, a voluptuous dream in an eclipse.
>
> The furniture takes elongated shapes, prostrate and languorous. Each piece seems to be dreaming, as if living in a state of trance, like vegetable and mineral things. The draperies speak an unvoiced language, like flowers and skies and setting suns [...]
>
> To what well-wishing demon am I indebted for being surrounded in this way by mystery and silence, peace and perfumes? What bliss? What we commonly call life, even at its most generous moments of euphoria has nothing to compare with this life of lives, which now I know and savour minute by minute and second after second.
>
> No – there are no more minutes, no seconds any more – Time has vanished away, Eternity reigns – an eternity of delights!
>
> But suddenly a terrible, heavy thump resounded on the door, and as in some hellish nightmare I felt as though I had just received a blow from a pick-axe, in the pit of my stomach.

And then a ghost came in – perhaps some bailiff come to torment me in the name of the law, or a shameless concubine to whine about her poverty and add the trivialities of her existence to the sufferings of my own, or some editor's errand-boy demanding the next instalment of copy.

The room which was heaven on earth, and the Idol, the Queen of Dreams – the Sylphide as Chateaubriand used to say – all that magic has vanished with the ghost's brutal hammering on the door.

How horrible – now I remember everything. Yes, this hovel, this home of everlasting boredom, is indeed my own. Look, there are the fatuous bits of junk, my dusty and chipped furniture; the fireless hearth with not even a glowing ember in the grate all fouled with spit; the dingy windows down which the rain has scrawled runnels in the grime; the manuscripts riddled with cross-outs or left half done; the calendar on which the evil days of reckoning are underlined in pencil […][59]

This is already beginning to look like familiar territory: the bracketing of everyday existence, the yearning for a form of suspended animation, the exclusion of others, and the inevitable incursion of change and decay; once again in the form of officious time, with its remorseless tread and its rap on the door. Both Dickens and De Quincey enter this backwater in time and space by withdrawing from the hubbub of the city into a place deserted by others; De Quincey imagines a street that has been emptied out and then makes it re-form, as in a dream or a story by Kafka, into a hiding place that fails in its purpose of staving off the

59 Charles Baudelaire, 'The Twofold Room' in *Poems in Prose, and La Fanfarlo*, translated by Francis Scarfe (London: Anvil Press Poetry, 1989), pp.37–9.

moment when the self is called to account. Dickens shows us his protagonist choosing internal exile in order to escape from others' stories into one of his own choosing. But both are returned to the narrative or dramatic structures that will carry them off into a future dividing them from their own projects.

In the case of Baudelaire, the overarching narrative structure is withheld; or rather, several possible narrative structures are hinted at, without being fully disclosed, and none is given priority over the others; the prose poem quarantines itself from what lies outside it, refuses to affiliate itself to a larger context, but then does little else besides refer to these extraneous things precisely as traces, shadows and echoes. It sets boundaries to itself in order not to attract the attention of the authorities; which is to say, the kind of power that is wielded by conventional forms of sense-making; but it then exhausts itself in imagining the various ways in which those boundaries might be breached. The prose poem can only hold its ground within a confined space; a space small enough to monitor and control. And the method of confinement, of tactical down-sizing was learned by Baudelaire during the greatly protracted task of translating De Quincey. De Quincey's ruminative prose was reined in and corralled; translation involved systematic paraphrase and deselection; which is to say that long passages were routinely summarised and reduced to a précis of themselves, while other passages were simply replaced with a Baudelairean mimicry of De Quinceyan style. This was not translation so much as adaptation, the production of a French simulacrum of De Quincey, that was not atypical of translation methods in use at the time.

And it was not atypical of De Quincey's own writing methods, or rather of his editing methods, since he constantly reordered and reconfigured his own texts, frequently dismembering them in order to redirect and redeploy fragments in alternative contexts, a practice that gave the excerpt partial independence and a somewhat estranged and more ghostly relation to context; the orphaned De Quinceyan paragraph may be seen as one of the formative gestures towards the evolution of the prose poem.

A certain amount of writing has been devoted to the intimate relationship between the prose poem and the city. Nikki Santilli, in her very busy study of the genre, relates the miniaturisation of literary form in the mid-nineteenth century to what she calls the diminution of space during the industrial age, pointing both to urban overcrowding and to what she describes as 'the gradual encroachment of the horizon.'[60] There is a persuasive neatness to this, although the same pressure results in a mania for detecting and establishing hidden connections between far-flung components of the urban system – revealing that it is one vast system – when evident connections are lacking; and the preferred mode of writing for this includes some of the longest novels in the language – while it might be said that the prose poem is one very significant symptom of a desire to cut connections, and shrink the horizon almost to an extent that makes it disappear altogether. Baudelaire's prose poem 'The Twofold Room' gives extra valency to the project of cutting connections by threatening to eclipse it with its double. One room resists the incursion of outside forces while the other succumbs to the pressure of other people's needs, but the two rooms are same room occupying two different sets of textual relations. The agents of entanglement bring with them unknown numbers of different

---

60 Nikki Santilli, *Such Rare Citings: The Prose Poem in English Literature* (London: Associated University Presses, 2002), p.185.

narrative threads that threaten to proliferate, on the Dickensian model, while the occupant of the room barricaded by his own aversion has only to glimpse one such thread in order to drop it altogether. The latter version of the room has the shape of the prose poem. Santilli traces the symbiosis of the prose poem and the city up to the very recent past, as far as Charles Tomlinson and Roy Fisher, but her conceptualisation of the urban environment remains tied to the conditions of the industrial age. When the twentieth century prose poem decides to predicate its own concept of the city, this can take a very different form, under the influence of a different awareness of the city made possible by aerial observation, which not only restores the city to its place within the horizon, but also encompasses it within the aerial photograph. This perspective on the city first becomes possible in the middle of the nineteenth century. Henry Mayhew's remarkable account of the appearance of London seen from a balloon, has him marvelling at the miniaturisation of the streets and buildings, and of the humans moving within and between them like the 'animalcules in cheese':

In the opposite direction to that in which the wind was insensibly wafting the balloon, lay the leviathan Metropolis, with a dense canopy of smoke hanging over it, and reminding one of the fog of vapour that is often seen steaming up from the fields at early morning. It was impossible to tell where the monster city began or ended, for the buildings stretched not only to the horizon on either side, but far away into the distance, where, owing to the coming shades of evening and the dense fumes from the million chimneys, the town seemed to blend into the sky, so that there was no distinguishing earth from heaven. The multitude of roofs that extended back from the foreground was positively like a dingy red sea, heaving in bricken billows, and the seeming waves rising up one after the other till the eye grew wearied with following them. Here and there we could distinguish little bare green patches of parks, and occasionally make out the tiny circular enclosures of the principal squares, though, from the height, these appeared scarcely bigger than wafers. Further, the fog of smoke that over-shadowed the giant town was pierced with a thousand steeples and pin-like factory-chimneys.

That little building, no bigger than one of the small china houses that are used for burning pastilles in, is Buckingham Palace – with St James's Park, dwindled to the size of a card table, stretched out before it. Yonder is Bethlehem Hospital, with its dome, now about the same dimensions as a bell.

Then the little mites of men, crossing the bridges, seemed to have no more motion in them than the animalcules in cheese; while the streets appeared more like cracks in the soil than highways, and the tiny steamers on the river were only to be distinguished by the thin black trail of smoke trailing after them.[61]

Mayhew's altitude is not quite high enough for him to be able to engross the whole of London, but in the twentieth century it would become possible to enclose entire cities within the modest framework of a photograph. Twentieth-century prose poems are not simply aerial views of course, but perhaps the visual homogenisation of the city has assisted the move towards encapsulating the city in terms of its pattern or structure, which the prose poet displays after hovering over its activity or discourse until the secret of its

---

61 Henry Mayhew and John Binny, 'The Criminal Prisons of London', *Illustrated London News*, 18 September, 1852.

operations and the defining aspects of its character should reveal themselves.

Italo Calvino's Invisible Cities consists entirely of descriptions of dozens of imaginary cities each of which has its own overall character that is revealed only when the narrator finds the correct detail with which to prise it open. This is the complete text of 'Cities and the Sky: 3':

> Those who arrive at Thekla can see little of the city, beyond the plank fences, the sackcloth screens, the scaffoldings, the metal armatures, the wooden catwalks hanging from ropes or supported by sawhorses, the ladders, the trestles. If you ask, 'Why is Thekla's construction taking such a long time?' the inhabitants continue hoisting sacks, lowering leaded strings, moving long brushes up and down, as they answer, 'So that its destruction cannot begin.' And if asked whether they fear that, once the scaffoldings are removed, the city may begin to crumble and fall to pieces, they add hastily, in a whisper, 'Not only the city.'
>
> If, dissatisfied with the answers, someone puts his eye to a crack in a fence, he sees cranes pulling up other cranes, scaffoldings that embrace other scaffoldings, beams that prop up other beams. 'What meaning does your construction have?' he asks. 'What is the aim of a city under construction unless it is a city? Where is the plan you are following, the blueprint?'
>
> 'We will show it to you as soon as the working day is over; we cannot interrupt our work now,' they answer.
>
> Work stops at sunset. Darkness falls over the building site. The sky is filled with stars. 'There is the blueprint,' they say.[62]

---

62 Italo Calvino, Invisible Cities (London: Vintage Books, 1997), p.115.

In one sense, this text simply extrapolates from the material reality of cities, that are never in a state of completion but always being added to, subtracted from, and repeatedly revised. But the materials of Thekla all have the aspect of an elaborate disguise, hiding the true nature of the city, which can only be perceived with the right angle of vision, the unobtrusive device that will reveal the principles of its construction. They mirror the textual strategies of Calvino's writing, withholding the clue that will lead the way out of the labyrinth, except that the clue leads to the understanding that the labyrinth is endless. Finding the keyhole, turning the key in the door and opening the door leads only to a *mise en abyme*.

Once again, the confinement of the prose poem, that favours the microscopic scrutiny of tiny details, is balanced against the awareness that there are entire constellations of similar details awaiting similar treatment. Perhaps the majority of Calvino's cities are flimsy and precarious structures, as if owning up to, and even parading, the fact that they are no more than imaginary, and seem to propose that all cities attain their identities only in the imaginary constructions of their inhabitants and visitors, each of whom invents a city different from all others.

Calvino's text comes to an end by drawing the veil of darkness over itself, as do all the texts of the *Invisible Cities* book, whether or not they mention their diurnal status, since each one is delivered as a daily report to Kubla Khan by the traveller Marco Polo, who may be describing actual places he has visited, but is much more likely to be inventing them, just as the historical Marco Polo has been credited with a fertile imagination, and the poetical Kubla Khan has been associated with the desire to build fantastical structures. Polo tells his stories to remain in the Khan's favours, just as Scheherezade returns every day to the task of delaying her own story's end. The prose poem lives on a day to day basis for a different reason, so as not to become caught up in a larger structure alien to its own purpose. Turgenev started writing prose poems in the 1860s and advised his readers to read them one a day, so as not to allow them to bleed into one another and coalesce.[63] What I want to end by arguing – although I haven't reached the end yet – is that the contemporary prose poem is far from resorting to the city as the ideal setting enabling it to accentuate and even dramatise its attempt to quarantine itself from the tyrannies of narrative – that in fact it is in contemporary nature writing, or one conspicuous strain of it, with its intervention into temporal and spatial measures far more immense than those of any city, that the need has been felt to create temporal and spatial lairs – to be territorial in perhaps every sense. From my point of view the best contemporary writing about nature actually domesticates it, in the process of estranging the domestic; as in the reined-in ruminations of Tim Dee's recent book, Four Fields:

Indoors, looked at from the field, seemed at best to be talk about life instead of life itself. Rather than living under the sun it fizzed – if it fizzed at all – parasitically or secondarily, with batteries, on printed pages, and in flickering images. I realised this around 1968 in my seven-year-old way. At the same time, however, I learned that I needed the indoor world to make the outdoors be something more than simply everything I wasn't. I saw it was true that indoor talk helped the outdoor world come alive and could of itself be living and lovely, too. Words about birds made birds live

63 Ivan Turgenev, Poems in Prose (London: Lindsay Drummond, 1945), p.vi.

as more than words. Jane Eyre, held inside by bad weather, takes Thomas Bewick's *History of British Birds* to the window and reads looking out into the wind and rain...

Without fields – no us. Without us – no fields. So it has come to seem to me. 'This green plot shall be our stage,' says Peter Quince in *A Midsummer Night's Dream*. Fields were there at our beginning and they are growing still. *Earth* half-rhymes with *life* and half-rhymes with *death*. Every day, countless incarnations of our oldest history are played out in a field down any road from wherever we are. Yet these acres of shaped growing earth, telling our shared story over and over, are so ordinary, ubiquitous and banal that we have – mostly – stopped noticing them as anything other than substrate or backdrop, the green crayon-line across the bottom of every child's drawing. For Walt Whitman, prairie-dreamer of the great lawn of men, grass fitted us and suited; it was a 'uniform hieroglyphic'. It grew and stood for us and, because it goes where we are, we tread where it grows. Yet because it meant everything it could easily mean nothing. It is in the nature of all commonplaces that they are overlooked, in both senses of the word: fields are everywhere but we don't see them for they are too familiar and homely; being the stage and not the show, they are trodden underfoot, and no one seeks them out, no one gives a sod.[64]

Dee's writing is all about scaling nature down by bringing inside the world outside, and by managing the relationship through a series of frames; moving outside the perimeters of the page, the screen, the window and the room by extending the principle of framing out into nature itself and restricting the field of vision to the vision allowed by the perimeters of the field. The field, with its hedgerow,

---

64 Tim Dee, *Four Fields* (London: Vintage Books, 2014), pp.2–3.

earthen bank or fence, is equivalent to Calvino's crack in the fence; an aperture through which to bring into focus nature's seemingly endless process of construction and dereliction. Dee's own emotional conviction is that life itself is found outdoors; that time spent indoors is a period of exile from the natural habitat; that life in a room is temporary imprisonment, it is where one exists in a protracted state of divided attention: 'reading looking out'. But his writing does almost the opposite; when his writing goes out into the field, it simply expands the measures of containment; it represents him looking out, and looking around, as if he is engaged in reading; his observations in the field stick to the arrangements on the page with edges defined by human history. Robert Macfarlane is engaged in a related activity, collecting the local glossaries for outdoor features and phenomena, in a range of different parts of the British archipelago. The reach of the dialect is the expanded field of community, whose 'talk about life' is what governs their attention to what lies around them: 'Without fields – no us. Without us – no fields.'

This stylistic parallelism, often involving symmetry and reversal, and alert to the echoing possibilities of rhyme and half-rhyme, gives the organisation of Dee's text the aspect of a set of adjacent units that are structurally related but self-contained, like a group of adjoining fields: 'Words about birds made birds live as more than words'; 'It grew and stood for us and, because it goes where we are, we tread where it grows'; 'Yet because it meant everything it could easily mean nothing.' The balance in these phrases and clauses, the assonance and alliteration, and the occasional use of a caesura-like turning point in the sentence, combine elements of several rhetorical and poetic traditions – imposing a vertical grid on top of the horizontal grid that normally controls our reading of a prose text.

This poetic drawing together of the elements of the text, so that they face inwards, strengthening the relations involved in the experience of reading the page, *especially* when these are concerned with looking out, is even more actively pursued in John Berger's remarkable text, ostensibly an essay, entitled 'Field':

Shelf of a field, green, within easy reach, the grass on it not yet high, papered with blue sky through which yellow has grown to make pure green, the surface colour of what the basin of the world contains, attendant field, shelf between sky and sea, fronted with a curtain of printed trees, friable at its edges, the corners of it rounded, answering the sun with heat, shelf on a wall through which from time to time a cuckoo is audible, shelf on which she keeps the invisible and intangible jars of her pleasure, field that I have always known, I am lying raised up on one elbow wondering whether in any direction I can see beyond where you stop. The wire around you is the horizon.

Remember what it was like to be sung to sleep. If you are fortunate, the memory will be more recent than childhood. The repeated lines of words and music are like paths. These paths are circular and the rings they make are linked together like those of a chain. You walk along these paths and are led by them in circles which lead from one to the other, further and further away. The field upon which you walk and upon which the chain is laid is the song.[65]

The first word of the first paragraph here introduces a collocation of vocabulary that we allocate in the first instance to the realm of metaphor: shelf, wallpaper, basin, curtain,

65 John Berger, 'Field', in *Why Look at Animals* (London: Penguin Books, 2009).

wall, jar. Just grouping these words together is enough to make the metaphorical application seem tenuous, and by the time we have reached the end of the first paragraph, in our first reading of the text, we have reassigned all these words to a literal function. At some point in our reading we hesitate between the literal and the metaphorical alternatives, and it is that hesitation which tells the truth about our dependence on frames and perimeters, on the various limitations we feel the need to impose on our assimilation of the world outdoors, on that enormous context always ready to swallow up our significance, not just as individuals, but as entire species.

The concept of the field seems always to be there, ready and waiting – 'attendant' – to such an extent that it seems 'I have always known it', which is to say, we have all always known it; our dependence on it such that we cannot see, and can only barely conceive of, what lies beyond, even though the evidence of our senses apart from vision interferes with our choice of horizon.

The prose poem is modernity's response not to an encroaching horizon but to our fear of the receding horizon, whose growing distance increases our share of the unknown. It is the circle we draw around our interactions with the world, in imitation of the literal wire that surrounds our fields, and the literal walls that compose our rooms: a circle drawn with the music of words; chains of words and concepts whose concentric rings repeat themselves in radiating out towards one text after another for at least the last one hundred and fifty years.

2016

The Eighth Hill of Rome

The Testaccio district in Rome is dominated by Monte Testaccio, a one-hundred-feet high, one-kilometre-square, pile of broken potsherds. This great mound of ceramic refuse, started in the first century BCE, was added to on a daily basis over the following four centuries. Co-existent with the Empire, it grew into a mass whose sheer bulk and consistency could not be reduced. Unlike the Empire, it did not fall. Pottery is an especially obdurate artefact, but every single piece of pottery in Monte Testaccio is of a particular sort – each fragment is a sherd of broken oil amphora.

Rome's greatest invention, apart from the Empire, was concrete. Everything went into concrete: lime and volcanic ash, chunks of rock, brick rubble, and lots of broken pottery – everything, in fact, except oil amphorae. Lime mixed with olive oil produces a soapy substance, and the Romans took steps to avoid aqueducts full of washing-up suds, temples with slippery steps, city gates foaming at the mouth, bubble-bath colosseums. Like concrete, the Empire was an amalgam with ingredients gathered from many different sources and bonded together. Just as Roman concrete could be stronger than rock, so the combination of racial and cultural elements made the empire seem indestructible. And yet, not far from its centre there lay Monte Testaccio, the eighth hill, the one built by human hands, a monument to non-integration. The makers of the Empire kept all the broken bits of oil amphorae away from their recycling centres. Paradoxically, when the imperial bonding agent passed its sell-by date and fell apart, Monte Testaccio held together.

In March of this year, I tried to find a way up it. A modern flight of steps had been constructed on the north east corner, but this lay behind a locked gate with a 'vietato accesso' sign attached to it. In the 1930s the mound was dressed up as a park but it has been closed for much of the time since World War Two, partly to protect it but also because the refuse of ancient commerce began to acquire an extra crust of debris from the modern heroin trade. As I write, activists known as 'Eighth Hill' are using change.org to press the Italian government for open access.

Testaccio has its followers. Entry denied, the connoisseur of history's leavings does not give up without a struggle. Eighth Hill addicts need their fix, and this is partly because the leavings in question hand down literally from ancient to modern fingertips the physical record of something still in daily use; something we know the feel of, the savour of — something whose density, rate of flow and soapiness are all thoroughly familiar. What's more, we still import it, or much of it, direct from the same place that supplied the bulk of the oil inside the Testaccio amphorae: Andalucia, which the Romans called Baetica. We are still inside that circuit, yet left outside the Testaccio ring-fence.

According to Pliny the Elder (Historia Naturalis, 17), the olive was the largest tree species in Baetica — so olives were big in every sense. Historians of the Roman economy have estimated olive oil consumption during the period of the Empire as twenty litres per person per year. In a city of one million, that certainly makes for a lot of empty oil containers, but it also makes clear the centrality of olive oil to Roman existence. As D.J. Mattingly puts it, in a review of studies of ancient oil production and distribution, 'the olive was (and is) fundamental in shaping the landscape, the way of life, the economy and the mentality of the Mediterranean' (Journal of Roman Archaeology 1 (1988) p.161). That parenthetical 'is' now stretches beyond the Mediterranean, since even the present-day inhabitants of Ultima Thule are now within the same — dare I say it — common market. Diet equals mentality. In our own case, you might say that olive oil lubricates a set of connections that have been in motion since literate culture began in Europe.

The inaugural European text, The Odyssey, is nothing if not Mediterranean, island-hopping, constantly embarking from one coastline to another, propelled by exile into a series of voyages across the Middle Sea. Britain's island status brings it closer and makes it more susceptible to this experience than the mainland culture of much of Europe. And surely the number of translations, adaptations and updated versions of The Odyssey is greater in English than in any other language.

The thesis of Barry Cunliffe's Facing the Ocean (2001) is that Neolithic and Bronze Age civilisations crested the sea-lanes and that coastal communities were key in the relay of artefacts and ideas. Nowadays, the same routes have been reawakened, forming escape-corridors for those desperate to flee barbarism. The seas bring peril, great risks, but also hope. The land is ring-fenced, unyielding, unmoved.

The ring-fence around Testaccio is no stand-in for the European laager, even though it runs close to that cordon sanitaire of symbols, the wall of the new Museum of Contemporary Art Testaccio, housed in an old slaughterhouse. The Eighth Hill also looks down on the Protestant Cemetery, where the remains of Keats and Shelley lie buried. The latter had written 'it might make one in love with death, to be buried in so sweet a place', although this was half a century before Testaccio morphed into the Roman Smithfield, lapped by the sounds and smells of industrial butchery.

The Testaccio you can visit now is all about the contemporary: presentness, living for the day – or rather, for the night. The hill is surrounded by bars and nightclubs – with names like Alibi, Radio Londra, Jungle Club, Orpheus, On the Rocks – cheek-by-jowl with butchers (still) and copy-shops. Thomas Hardy thought up a poem nearby, one of several written in Rome during 1887, on the shape-shifting nature of time and the collapsing of the present and past into one. Despite the perdurability of its ruins, nothing in Rome really lasts compared to the 'matchless singing' of the poets. Hardy had in mind Keats and Shelley. He did not have in mind the unmatched volume of Testaccio's nightclub music when darkness falls. This racket seems to threaten another kind of collapse altogether. It fills the air like a sonic pile-driver – one can sense it pumping noise pollutants into all the voids and cavities formed by thousands of layers of smashed amphorae, so that every part of the hill vibrates.

The ancient disposal teams showed a predilection for order in the very act of destruction. All around the perimeter of the hill, the amphora shards are stacked neatly in a series of terraces. Even rubbish was an engineering project. On the surface at least. The interior of the heap was a morass, into which an unending landslip of ceramic trash was released. Like the built structure of the Empire, the spectacle of order was a repeat performance, a fundamental routine, but everything behind this facade was subject to continuous structural change. At a certain point, the most recent arrivals proved in some way anomalous, refractory, inimical, to a degree that threatened the integrity of the whole, and the aggregates of Empire and Testaccio both stopped growing. The Empire went into panic reverse mode, recalling the troops and abandoning the edgelands, those provinces that had never looked at home in the invader's team strip. Britannia went its own way in 410; Spain finally in 472.

I left Rome on 24 March 2017, the day before the Consilium, the ancient-sounding meeting of EU leaders on the sixtieth anniversary of the signing of the Treaty of Rome in 1957. This birthday for the launching of the EU was something of a shipwreck. The twenty-seven Heads of State pronounced that 'our union is undivided and indivisible'. Not so indivisible, apparently, that it did not also call for 'even greater unity and solidarity amongst us'. While they fiddled, Rome flared up all over the place. The protests in the streets were so violent that a buffer zone was set up around the Capitoline Hill while the anniversary talks were underway. Apart from the five 'authorised' demonstrations, there were also flashpoints involving trade unionists and anarchists on the left, and groups such as Forza Nuova ('Give Rome back to the Romans') and Fratelli d'Italia on the right. There were running battles up and down streets where, earlier on, I had idled among the parked-up Lambrettas, cutlery shops, gutter-cats, potted olive trees and jaded ruins of the ancients.

Two days later, on the 27 March 2017, the Italian police announced the finding of an enormous illegal toxic waste dump filling a quarry in Aprilia, a few miles south of Rome. Which made me wonder, whether a Monte Aprilia would say as much about our own economy and culture as Monte Testaccio had done for the Imperium Romanum. The one would be no less international than the other; and if, statistically speaking, there was to be a British section, it would consist of chemicals, fertilisers, nitrogen compounds, plastics, pharmaceuticals, synthetic rubber, petrol, gas and cars – because these are the UK's main exports to Italy. Much more toxic would be the non-degradable excess of Brexit propaganda, the one-hundred-feet-high, one-kilometre-square, mound of broken promises. And, sitting on top, would be a still-quivering set of great yellow donkey teeth that once belonged to some forgotten demagogue. Let's imagine that analysis of root and enamel from these teeth to determine the levels of oxygen and strontium isotopes would not give a clear indication of geographical origin, owing to European-wide patterns of trade and consumption. Our diet now does not have a passport. You are what you eat.

2017

Acknowledgements

Extracts from an early version of the first section of Grimspound were published under the title 'from Grimspound" in Contour Lines: New Responses to Landscape in Word and Image, ed. Neil Wenborn and M.E.J.Hughes (Cambridge: Salt Publishing, 2009), pp.78–85.

'Knife' was first published in PN Review, 222 (March-April 2015), pp.55–6.

'Soluble Culture' was first published in The Kenyon Review (Summer/Fall, 2003), pp.72–7.

'Walking with Sebald' was first published in Leviathan Quarterly, No.6 (December, 2002), pp.56–8.

'Their Master's Voice; the Megaphones of Prague' was first published in Frieze (Issue 78, October 2003), p.70.

'End of the Line' was first published as an image-text collaboration with Marc Atkins in London: from Punk to Blair, ed. Andrew Gibson and Joe Kerr (London: Reaktion Books, 2003), pp.445–57.

'A Wild Nursery for the Arts: the Site of the V&A' was first published in V&A Magazine, number 5 (Winter 2004/5), pp.56–64.

'Atkins / Warsaw' was first published as 'Warsaw by Marc Atkins' in The Liberal, Issue 7 (February/March, 2006), pp.66–7.

'Lares et Penates' was first published as 'Deep Space: the Studio of Anselm Kiefer' in Art Review, Vol.LVI (July, 2005), pp.80–2.

'Spatial Utopias: Ilya and Emilia Kabakov' was first published in Art Review, Vol.LVII (October, 2005), pp.106–09.

'A Perfect Likeness: Nineteenth Century Casts' was first published in V&A Magazine, Number 9 (Spring, 2006), pp.56–61.

'Not Him' was first published as 'Not Him: Nauman, Guston, Beckett', in Poetry Review Vol.96:2 (Summer, 2006), pp.113–14.

'Birth of a Mountain' was first published in The Warwick Review Vol.1, No.1 (March, 2007), pp.139–43.

'Light: A Total Installation' was first published in Light [exhibition catalogue] (Winchester Cathedral, 2007), pp.3–5.

'Margaret Tait' was first published in *Art Monthly*, Number 310 (October, 2007), p.39.

'The Real Avant-Garde' was first published in *A Room to Live In: a Kettle's Yard anthology*, ed. Tamar Yoseloff (Cambridge: Salt Publishing, 2007), pp.70–3.

'Sutton Hoo: The Shipping Forecast' was first published in *The Warwick Review*, Vol.2, No.2 (June, 2008), pp.28–32.

'Shot By Both Sides' was first published in *Medals of Dishonour*, ed. Philip Attwood and Felicity Powell (London: The British Museum Press, 2009), pp.33–7.

'Assymetries in the Bush' was first published in *Angelaki: Journal of the Theoretical Humanities*, special issue on ecopoetics, ed. Kate Fagan, John Kinsella and Peter Minter, Vol.14, No.2 (2009), pp.85–91.

'The Folding Telescope and Many Other Virtues of Bruno Schulz' was first published in *The Kenyon Review* Vol.XXXIII, No.3 (Summer 2011), pp.153–66.

'Vacant History' was first published as a text and image collaboration with Marc Atkins in Marc Atkins and Rod Mengham, *Still Moving* (London: Veer Publications, 2014), pp.67–8.

'Underworld' was written during an artist's residency at 'Les Recollets', Paris, in 2013.

'Doris Salcedo and the Philosophy of Furniture' was delivered as a lecture at the Guggenheim Museum, New York, in October 2015.

'Steve McQueen's *Static* and the State We're In' was first published as 'The Poetic Nature of *Static*' in Rachel Wells (ed.) *In Focus: Static 2009 by Steve McQueen*, Tate Research Publication (2017), http://www.tate.org.uk/research/publications/in-focus/static-steve-mcqueen/poetic-nature,

'The Prose Poem' was first published as 'A Genealogy of the Prose Poem' in *Countertext* 3.2, ed. James Corby and Ivan Callus (2017), pp.176–86.

'The Eighth Hill of Rome' was first published in *LRB Blog*, 6 September 2017, www.lrb.co.uk/blog/2017/09/06/rod-mengham/the-eighth-hill-of-rome.